PLAN
COMMIT
WIN

Enjoy the journey!

− P.H.

PLAN
COMMIT
WIN

90 DAYS TO CREATING A FUNDABLE STARTUP

The Process I Used to Raise $200 Million and Drive $2 Billion in M&A

PATRICK HENRY

QuestFusion
PUBLISHING

ISBN 978-0-692-86812-6

Published by QuestFusion Publishing

Cover design by Chin Yee Lai

Interior layout by John H. Matthews, BookConnectors.com

Production coordinated by Patrick Henry and John H. Matthews, BookConnectors.com

To receive a free monthly e-mail newsletter from the author on how to succeed as an entrepreneur in the digital age, subscribe at www.questfusion.com/contact-us/

Table of Contents

Acknowledgments

Any book, including this one, takes a lot of people to make it happen, but I would like to highlight a few individuals who made special contributions.

Amanda Henry is my partner, best friend, and creative sounding board. She provided the encouragement for me to develop my online consulting platform and start blogging about my experience as a startup CEO. The feedback that I received from my blog and published articles was invaluable in creating this book. Amanda also provided a lot of encouragement and support when I made the decision to write this book, including a substantial amount of understanding during the long and sometimes frustrating process. As an engineer, some people believe that math is my first language and English my second, even though I grew up in the American heartland. Amanda has been awesome throughout the writing process, reading and proofreading endless draft copies, providing insight, and helping me with words so that the book is more accessible and readable by a larger audience.

Since I am an engineer and business executive, I have spent nearly my entire career working for and building technology companies. When I started QuestFusion in early 2015, I basically changed careers from being a "product guy" to a "professional services person." It was a really big change, but it was essential to creating the contents and testing the ideas presented in this book. A few key people have been very helpful in this process, including my friend and business attorney, Jeremy Glaser, from Mintz-Levin. Jeremy is not only an attorney; he is a specialist in corporate law as it relates to venture capital and startups. Leland Sandler, a successful executive coach, has been valuable both as a mentor and friend. My long-term mentor, former business executive and venture capitalist Umesh Padval, has also been a great sounding board to me, as he has been for the last 20 years. Rory Moore, the CEO of EvoNexus, a technology incubator, and the founder of a couple other startups, has been a great friend and mentor during the process of working with entrepreneurs and creating my video blog, The Real Deal…What Matters, and has provided key insights about working with early stage companies. Tim Owens, who runs Life Lounge San Diego, has been a great networking partner who has connected me to many terrific entrepreneurs and business owners, who have in turn provided great insight about the challenges of entrepreneurship outside of the technology world. During my MBA program in the early 1990s, I was very fortunate to develop a strong relationship with Ken Merchant, PhD, a professor at the University of Southern California, and the former Dean of Accountancy at that school. I worked as a summer intern for Ken as a business case writer, and this was the primary catalyst for me to do more writing throughout my business career, which provided a foundation for blogging and the eventual writing of this book. Ken was also on the board of directors at Entropic, and has remained a great sounding board and mentor to this day. Interestingly, my golf coach, Geoff Goldstein, has also been a great referral partner. He helps me with golf, and I help him with business and entrepreneurship.

Self-publishing, if done correctly, is a very complex process. I suppose that is why we still have a publishing industry. Since I am a business executive and adviser, I do not have a publishing background or any previous experience publishing a book. I did a lot of research on self-publishing, traditional publishing, and Indy publishing before making the decision about how to produce this book. I read many articles and had discussions with other authors. One tremendous resource in this process was Publishing 101 by Jane Friedman. Jane also has a really terrific blog about writing and publishing that has been very helpful. Although I have never met Jane, she has been a big help in getting this book produced in a professional way. Special thanks also go out to Christine Moore, from New York Editors. Christine looked at the book from a different angle and did what I try to do with my clients by asking, "How would an average entrepreneur better understand the concepts in this book?" I also owe special thanks to my publicist Jane Wesman, the president and founder of Jane Wesman Public Relations, who has been in the book publishing industry for over 30 years. Jane has provided key insights about the writing and publishing process that were essential for me to get this book produced in a professional way. Henry DeVries, the author of Marketing with a Book and founder of Indie Books International, was also a great resource for ideas on how to publish a book as a business adviser. John H. Matthews of BookConnectors.com did the interior design of the book and helped coordinate production, and Chin Yee Lai did the cover design. The goal for me was to deliver a book with the same quality standards as a top publishing house.

As part of the process of launching this book, I conducted a Kickstarter campaign to generate interest and awareness for the book. It was a tremendous success, and we raised 240 percent of the funding goal over 30 days from 120 people in 10 different countries. Key contributors to this campaign included Oren Klaff, the author of Pitch Anything. Other key contributors included Bhenam Analui, PhD, the founder and CEO of Abtum; Olin Hyde, the founder and CEO of LeadCrunch; Bryan Renaud, the founder and CEO of Podify; and Avi Madisetti, the founder of MyTech LLC. All of these gentlemen are also clients and have become good friends. I learn as much from them as they do from me. My best friend since high school, John Whitener, was also a key contributor to the Kickstarter campaign. John and his wife Amy are both entrepreneurs and business owners. John was named one of the "Top 30 Under 30" business executives in St. Louis, and has continued to pursue entrepreneurial ventures throughout his career. Itzhak Gurantz, the founding CEO of Entropic, has also been a tremendous supporter and mentor to me for over a decade.

Of course no thank you would be complete without thanking my parents, Charlie and Ann Henry, who taught me about hard work, being honest, unconditional love, and caring for the people around me. I also have to thank my kids, Austin, Ella, Preston, Shea and Kyen, for the lessons that they teach me every day.

Foreword

Why does one business plan receive millions of dollars in funding, yet another plan (that is very similar or even *better*) get passed over?

Truth is, most startups that wish to become growth companies uniformly make the same mistakes. If you meet 100 companies that are seeking investment or looking to grow rapidly, then you'll hear the same thing 95 times, "*We're the first company to create an 'xyz thing' and our 'abcdefg product features' are going to revolutionize the market.*"

Then, the CEO will deliver the punchline: "Although we're just starting out, you can see on slide 29, that by the end of year-three we're making huge amounts of money."

Slide 29?

Year three?

That's a punchline that has no punch.

First, there about a million things the investor wants to know about your company TODAY before he will buy into your vision of The Exciting Future That Is Three Years From Now. And these investors don't want to sit through 29 slides to hear all about it.

Sadly, most companies present a plan they *think* investors want to see. They dutifully fill out slides titled *competition, market size* and *use-of-funds*. In fact, right on Sequoia's home page, THEY TELL YOU what to put on those slides (*competition, market size, use of funds* … etc.)

Yes, of course, Patrick Henry knows what you should put on those slides too. But his version may not be what you think.

For certain, he knows how to make difficult concepts easy to understand and hard facts easy reading. But that doesn't make funding certain. And he often will take responsibility of helping investors understand the financeability of a company -- by simplifying the company's most important and complex issues (for example, it almost always helps to lead with the problem, not the solution and *most plans get this backwards.*)

But that doesn't make funding certain either.

So where does certainty come from?

I suggest my start-ups use **PLAN COMMIT WIN** to improve their chance of success because Patrick doesn't think just in terms of *what you should tell an investor* – or in terms of slides or spreadsheets or org charts.

He thinks in the same terms that investors do: what's the *plan*. You'll notice the first word in the title of his book is PLAN.

In his world, where checks get written, companies grow quickly and move on to gain larger customers and larger rounds of investment, *you need a plan that is likely to work* ... not one you made-up while filling in template slides downloaded from Sequoia's website.

You need a financial model that looks pretty similar to other funded companies' financial models when they were at your same stage (think: Dropbox wasn't always a 1,000 employee tech company and not long ago they were a three person startup with a beta product and a short business plan, about 12 slides. You probably want to look more like them than you realize.)

And as Patrick writes in this book, you need to leave the investor with much more than a plan because there are things investors and buyers want to know that cannot be put so easily on a slide, but nevertheless must be made clear, obvious and inarguable: Why *this* team? Why *now*, what is *changing* in the market and what *exactly* is happening in your company when your spreadsheet model starts to "hockey-stick."

I have seen thousands of start-up companies give a pitch for investment. While they have many facts, formulas, features and forecasts ... I wish they all had spent time with this book, **PLAN COMMIT WIN**.

Here you'll learn that a plan doesn't show how you become a multi-national billion-dollar company in five years. No one cares about *that* story.

A plan communicates how all these things you plan on doing *will work together in year one*, and then year two. How you'll actually do the things you say you'll do. And why, amidst the other 10,000 options an investor has to invest in, your company, your product, your plan is *the right one to invest in*.

There are many people who can help you put slides together. Advisers. Attorneys. Coaches. Friends. They will solemnly, laboriously and obediently make for you lists of *things you're supposed to have* ... like *market size* and *pricing matrix*. But there are few people who can help produce a useful, believable, and actionable plan that you can COMMIT to. And that investors can finance because they believe you can win.

For this reason, it's my pleasure to introduce, endorse and recommend this book.

Oren Klaff
Author, Pitch Anything
Managing Partner, Intersection Capital

Introduction

I have spent the past two decades building, running, buying and selling businesses, and the last couple of years consulting dozens of startup and growth stage company founders and CEOs on their strategies and funding plans. Over this time, I have observed a common set of reasons that startups struggle and fail, as well as a consistent set of factors that make startup companies successful.

My experience has exposed me to solutions to many of the most persistent issues that startups face. As I wrote in an article for *Entrepreneur*, "Why Some Startups Succeed (and Why Most Fail)," I felt that I could be helpful to entrepreneurs looking to build and grow their companies – so I started a company called QuestFusion to provide strategic guidance to startups. As I met with dozens of entrepreneurs seeking guidance and investment, I noticed a recurring pattern. Most of these entrepreneurs had deep product knowledge, but lacked some of the fundamental knowledge and experience of how to build a successful business and effectively raise capital. My curiosity around startup success and failure eventually compelled me to do some in-depth investigation around this topic. I wondered whether research studies out there showed why startups succeed and fail. While I found several articles filled with unsubstantiated opinions, I did unearth a few sources with some hard research around the topic.

Why Companies Fail

According to an article in *FastCompany*, "Why Most Venture Backed Companies Fail," 75 percent of venture-backed startups fail. This statistic is based on a *Harvard Business School* study by Shikhar Ghosh. In a study by *Statistic Brain*, "Startup Business Failure Rate by Industry," the failure rate of companies based in the U.S. after five years was over 50 percent, and over 70 percent after 10 years. This study also looked at the company leadership reasons for business failure. It gave a list of four main reasons for failure, and some sub-categories within those. It also gave a list of 12 leading management mistakes. This research-based analysis confirmed some of my observations. I bucket the *Statistic Brain* findings into seven key reasons entrepreneurs experienced business failure:

1. Lack of focus
2. Lack of motivation, commitment and passion
3. Too much pride resulting in an unwillingness to see or listen
4. Taking advice from the wrong people
5. Lacking good mentorship
6. Lack of general and domain specific business knowledge: finance, operations, and marketing
7. Raising too much money too soon

All of these errors have a common thread: they stem from weakness in the entrepreneur's decision-making abilities and general business knowledge.

In another study, *CB Insights* looked at post-mortems of 101 startups to compile a list of the "Top 20 Reasons Startups Fail" – with a focus on company level reasons for failure. This list is instructive, but each of these reasons is due to a failure in leadership at some level. The top nine most significant from this study are:

1. No market need for what the company offered
2. Ran out of cash
3. Not the right team
4. Got out-competed
5. Pricing/cost issue
6. Poor product
7. Need/lack business model
8. Poor marketing
9. Ignoring customers

All of these are business and team related issues, even the ones that relate to the product. Issues like these are always tied to a leader's ability to build a strong team and drive a business model and business thought process and discipline. Even if running out of money is the ultimate reason for failure, other factors have always led up to this result.

Why Startups Succeed

The next thing I did was to look for sources of information on why businesses were successful. I found a research study from *Harvard Business School*, "Performance Persistence in Entrepreneurship," which suggests that serial entrepreneurs with subsequent success are more likely to have success in the future – and that the best VCs are good at picking serial entrepreneurs. However, that really did not answer my question about the **qualities** of the entrepreneur.

The best comprehensive research I could find that helped to answer the "reasons for success" question was from the *Ecommerce Genome by Compass's* "Startup Genome" report, which looked at 650 internet startups. Though tech industry specific, this research was still very instructive – and highlighted 14 indicators of success. Some of the 14 were a bit redundant, which you will find if you review the report yourself – but this analysis also confirmed some of my observations. I bucket these 14 indicators into nine key factors for success:

1. Founders are **driven by impact** – resulting in passion and commitment
2. **Commitment to stay the course** and stick with a chosen path
3. Willingness to **adjust,** but not constantly adjusting
4. **Patience and persistence** due to the timing mismatch of expectations and reality
5. Willingness to **observe, listen, and learn**
6. Develop the right **mentoring** relationships
7. Leadership with **general and domain specific** business knowledge
8. Implementing "**Lean Startup**" principles: Raising just enough money in a funding round to hit the next set of key milestones
9. Balance of **technical and business knowledge,** with necessary technical expertise in product development

Are the Reasons for Success the *Opposite* of those for Failure?

There are things that you must possess to be a successful entrepreneur, but they will not guarantee success. That said, it stands to reason that if you fixed the reasons for business failure, you would at least improve your chances of success. So, I decided to look at a side-by-side comparison of the reasons for failure and the factors for success.

If you look at both the reasons for failure and the factors for success, clearly commitment to a plan is key. This, of course, implies having a plan. This contrasts with the study of startup failures that had a lack of focus and the wrong team. Having commitment and focus does not mean that you are completely inflexible, but it takes significant and drastic feedback to cause you to alter your course. This is why the most successful companies have no more than one or two pivots. Do not think of every minor business adjustment as a pivot. Successful companies constantly learn and adapt based on customer and market feedback. A true pivot is a change in course or direction that results in a material change in the **product-market strategy** and the associated resource allocation of the company. The resource changes are usually dramatic in product development, product management or marketing, or some combination of the three. According to *Forbes*, the most legendary pivot in social media history is the transformation of Odeo into Twitter. Odeo began as a network where people could find and subscribe to podcasts, but the founders feared the company's demise when iTunes began taking over the podcast niche. After giving the employees two weeks to come up with new ideas, the company decided to make a drastic change and run with the idea of a status-updating micro-blogging platform conceived by Jack Dorsey and Biz Stone.

The next set of reasons for business failure is a lack of passion, commitment and motivation. Nearly every entrepreneur, business coach, consultant, adviser, newscaster, investor and industry analyst talks about passion. Steve Jobs is still quoted all the time about this. It is probably becoming cliché and overused at this point. What I like about the "Startup Genome" report is that it goes to the root of the passion. People who are successful believe in what they are doing. The successful entrepreneur feels that they can make an impact and a difference in the world. There is so much inertia and negativity around getting a startup off the ground, much less getting it to "escape velocity," or the ability for your company to be consistently profitable and no longer reliant on infusions of outside capital. If you do not have this deep-seated commitment to making an impact, you will surely give up. Successful entrepreneurs are competitive. They play to win, and they hate to lose. This trait may present itself differently with different personality types, but I have never met a successful entrepreneur who does not have a competitive spirit and a will to win.

The next reason for failure is too much pride, resulting in an unwillingness to see or listen. Contrast this with the successful entrepreneur's willingness to observe, listen and learn. The next factor goes hand-in-hand with learning. Entrepreneurs who take advice from the wrong people and lack good mentorship frequently fail. Successful entrepreneurs develop the right mentoring relationships. Mentorship is critically important to business success, and it has played a huge role in my own career success. Just because you are willing to learn does not mean that you are willing to seek a mentor and listen to their guidance, but it sure helps! One of the key factors in selecting a mentor is finding someone with the time and willingness to listen. They also need to have empathy, but a willingness to deliver tough messages. Other key factors include a personality and a teaching style that is compatible with yours. By the way, I am not advocating that you take every piece of advice and guidance from your mentors, but if you have selected strong mentors that have the significant domain, technical or business expertise, you should at least thoughtfully consider what they have to say. Otherwise, why have them around as a mentor? A lot of being a good mentee boils down to humility. It's one of those things which, when you think you have it, you do not, and it is essential to being coachable. One of my favorite stories about successful mentorship is from Eric Schmidt, the former CEO of Google. When Schmidt was hired as CEO of Google in 2001, Google board member, early investor and renowned venture capitalist John Doerr suggested that Schmidt might benefit from a session with Bill Campbell, who was the former Chairman and former CEO of Intuit, another consumer-facing technology company. "My initial reaction was 'I don't need any help,'" said Schmidt, in a 2008 profile of Campbell in *Fortune*.

However, Schmidt quickly changed his mind as Campbell reorganized the company's engineering and product teams, helped build Google's board, and defused internal political problems. "His contribution to Google – it is literally not possible to overstate. He essentially architected the organizational structure," Schmidt said.

Successful startups are successful businesses. It therefore stands to reason that you need to establish and implement solid fundamental business principles and practices to improve your chances of success. Entrepreneurs who fail lack general and domain specific business knowledge: finance, operations, and marketing. They also frequently lack a well-thought-through business model. This is typically a result of not understanding the market and the competitive landscape, pricing and cost issues, a poorly defined product for the market need, poor marketing, and ignoring customer comments. By contrast, successful startups have leadership with general and domain specific business knowledge. These companies have a balance of technical and business knowledge, with necessary technical expertise in product development. They also have strong teams. Many technical founders fall in love with their product idea and consciously or unconsciously believe that if they build a better mousetrap, the world will beat a path to their door. However, both the success and failure studies show that you need leadership in the company with general and domain-specific business knowledge to be successful.

Does this mean that a technical founder cannot be successful as a CEO? No, it does not. A classic example is Dr. Irwin Jacobs, the co-founder and founding CEO of Qualcomm, the company that developed the dominant technology used in cell phones and mobile devices today. Dr. Jacobs is a brilliant engineer and former professor at MIT and the University of California, San Diego. However, he also has a brilliant business mind and a lot of business knowledge. Before Qualcomm, Dr. Jacobs ran another technology company, MA-Com, so he had business experience and knowledge before forming Qualcomm. He also surrounded himself with a strong management team. There are many other examples of this success formula, but there are more where there is a seasoned businessperson who has domain expertise leading the company, and a strong technical team driving product development. Steve Jobs (Apple, NeXT, and Pixar) is the classic example of a founder with strong business knowledge and skills. Meg Whitman (eBay) and Eric Schmidt (Google) are great examples of CEOs who were brought into companies at an early stage to complement an exceptional team of technical founders.

Startup success is also about raising the right amount of money. Venture capital-backed companies that fail typically raise too much money too soon, or they do not raise money at all due to a poor business model. Successful startups typically raise just enough money in a funding round to hit the next set of key milestones. These milestones are typically very clear and well understood by the team. The team is focused on accomplishing these key milestones, and they usually result in risk mitigation and a step-function increase in valuation for the company. Having a clear and realistic idea of how long things take, setting intermediate milestones for every 12 to 18 months, and raising just enough money to get to the next set of key milestones, is not only important to capital efficiency, it is also important for success. Apart from the amount of capital, successful startups are usually good stewards of whatever money they raise, and they operate lean.

An Exclusive Club

Interestingly, according to the *Kauffman Institute*, in its article "The Constant: Companies that Matter," the pace at which the United States produces $100-million companies has been stable over the last 20 years despite changes in the economy. As the study states, "Anywhere from 125 to 250 companies per year (out of roughly 552,000 new employer firms) are founded in the United States that reach $100 million in revenues." My former company, Entropic, achieved this status. How do you become part of that club? You need some luck and a good sense of timing. However, as the Roman philosopher Seneca said, "Luck is what happens when preparedness meets opportunity."

Beyond that, you need a plan, persistence, perseverance, a willingness to be flexible, and a world-class team. You also need to be frugal, bright, and cultivate strong mentors. The best way to do all these things well and efficiently is to follow the systematic process outlined in this book where you plan, commit, track results, promote accomplishments and raise the necessary capital, or "fuel in the tank," to drive the growth of your startup.

What is This Book All About?

PLAN COMMIT WIN is intended to be a step-by-step guide to building a fundable business plan and pitch. It will outline the process that I have used to provide structured guidance to dozens of startup companies, and to launch and fund half a dozen successful businesses. By following this process, you will establish a strong foundation for your company, increase your chances of receiving funding from the right investors, and create a flourishing business. Seeking out a strong business mentor – someone who has domain expertise in your vertical markets and knowledge about running and funding businesses that are complementary to your areas of expertise – will improve your chances of success even more.

I wrote this book for entrepreneurs, company founders, and startup CEOs looking to raise outside capital. The information I provide should be especially helpful for first time entrepreneurs, technical founders, and serial entrepreneurs who have not yet had their first success. Significant parts of the book are also relevant for small to midsize business owners who have domain expertise in their area of specialization, but lack some of the business fundamentals needed to successfully launch and grow their businesses.

This book's key components outline the exact process that I have used to build successful businesses, raise over $200 million in equity capital for my companies, execute in over $2 billion in M&A transactions, and take a company from pre-product and pre-revenue to a successful IPO and eventually a $1 billion valuation. These tactics are essential to running any startup business or growth company, and getting it funded. I hope you find this book to be instructive, somewhat entertaining, and helpful in establishing your business and attracting the needed capital to grow your company. I love working with entrepreneurs, and hope the guidance and experiences that I share here will help you to become one of the next great startup success stories.

CHAPTER 1

The Hierarchy of Raising Capital

You are likely more than aware of this by now, but it bears repeating: building and running a successful startup is *hard work*. It takes tenacity, focus, passion, patience, perseverance, planning, and promotion. Some of the most critical elements include setting the vision, building the strategy, driving your marketing and product development programs, and raising growth capital for your company.

In my discussions with dozens of entrepreneurs over the years, I frequently ask, "What do you lose sleep over?" The most consistent answer is "Raising my next funding round." This is understandable. Having sufficient cash for product development and driving the growth of the business is one of the most important jobs of a startup CEO. In my experience, there is a hierarchy of requirements for raising outside capital for your company.

Figure 1.1 - Hierarchy for Raising Capital

At the base of a fundable business is a strong idea, which needs to be fleshed out during the ideation stage of a company. This book outlines a screening process for smart ideation. Next, as you work through your product positioning, you need to work through a strategic planning process. Ideation and strategic planning work hand-in-hand to establish a strong foundation for a successful startup company. Once you have these foundational elements, you can develop an annual operating plan and budget. These tools are used to run the company, and track progress against milestones. The annual operating plan and other elements of the strategic plan serve as the contents of a business plan you can use with investors to tell your story and the story of your company; who you are and why you will be successful. Investors will also be looking at your team and your track record. The team and how you execute are key "proof points" that you do what you say, and your team has the capabilities to execute on the plan. As Morris Chang, the founder and chairman of Taiwan Semiconductor Manufacturing Company (TSMC) and the father of the fab-less semiconductor industry, the business model where chip companies outsource manufacturing, said: "Without strategy, execution is aimless. Without execution, strategy is useless." This statement embodies an enormous amount of wisdom that should be heeded by every entrepreneur. Next in the hierarchy is the investor presentation and pitch deck. All the key contents of a pitch can be found in the business plan. The other element of the pitch is the human element. Investors invest in companies with great businesses, teams that they feel can execute, and leadership that they trust. Your personal credibility and integrity will be judged every time you are in front of prospective investors. The types of preparation I describe in this book are essential in building the required relationships to get your company funded. If you do all these things, you will get to the prize, the dollar sign at the top of the pyramid. It may be euros, pounds, rubles, or yen, but you will get the necessary fuel to run and grow your business.

Most companies stall from the beginning, and are not able to raise cash for a variety of reasons. Perhaps they lack critical building blocks, which we discuss throughout this book, or it might be that the entrepreneur simply fails to instill confidence in prospective investors. What is truly unfortunate is that many of these failures could have been success stories if they just had the right guidance, planning capability, team building, and product positioning sense.

All first-time entrepreneurs lack experience in obtaining outside capital – it's just the nature of running a business for the first time! Even some second-time entrepreneurs have never raised a funding round. It's nothing to be ashamed or embarrassed about – and the good news is that it's certainly not a show-stopper for getting your company funded.

However, this absence of experience means that many entrepreneurs are in desperate need of solid guidance. Sometimes they are prideful and refuse to seek any advice. Other times they look in the wrong places for guidance, frequently turning to family members that do not have specific technical or domain knowledge. They often get advice from well-meaning friends with no experience of raising capital as a startup CEO. They do not want to pay for guidance from experienced professionals; after all, they are looking forward to raising money, not spending money. Some go to investment bankers who are willing to work on a "success fee" basis and who say they will make introductions to the right investors, but many

VCs do not like working with investment bankers – they prefer working directly with company CEOs and the management team. In an effort to create an inspiring presentation, some entrepreneurs hire graphic artists, or even a consultant to prepare a business plan or executive summary, but even the most attractive presentation will not get investors interested in their companies if they do not have substance. They may study things on the internet or read blogs from famous VCs and Angel inventors, but they really do not know whom they should trust, and they sometimes are not even sure what they need. Many may not be aware that a hierarchy for raising capital even exists, or perhaps they have a sense of this and know that they lack certain building blocks, but are not sure exactly what those are – or which ones they need to ascend to the top. The key building blocks for ascending the funding pyramid are what *PLAN COMMIT WIN* is all about.

I have listened to well over 100 startup presentations in my career. Many company presentations are missing at least one or two elements of the pyramid, while many others do not even have a well-formulated plan. In a recent example, I was at a pitch session of a local Angel investor group. Angel investors are high net worth individuals that make investments in startup companies. After the pitch session, which included presentations from six companies that were prescreened before the meeting, there was a private discussion with only the prospective investors. Even though these were screened presentations, representing the most promising business ideas that group had seen in the last month, the presentations still had significant issues. Most of the comments were about "building blocks" missing in the presentation that are described in *PLAN COMMIT WIN*, such as an understanding of the target market, target customers, competitive landscape, revenue projections, and market model. I commonly heard things during the discussion like, "I don't think he knows what he's talking about"; "It seemed like she was making stuff up about her market size"; "I still don't understand how they make money"; "I get a sense that there is an opportunity here, but she didn't do a good job qualifying it." Other comments related to trust and the credibility of the entrepreneurs, and included things like: "He really doesn't strike me as someone I could trust to watch my kids for a few hours, much less running a company." In almost all cases, these comments stem from a lack of preparation or knowledge on the part of the entrepreneur. This is a common situation.

Since these entrepreneurs do not have a way to diagnose the problem, they struggle to figure out how to fix it. They know that they have an amazing product with an incredible value proposition – and that they could launch an incredible business if they could only get the required funding. Since they do not realize *what* they are missing, they do not know where to begin.

Building a successful startup is about assembling a team, innovating and adjusting your ideas, planning a course, executing that plan, delivering results, promoting accomplishments, and having enough money, or "fuel in the tank," to drive your growth – then, repeating the process over the next planning cycle. My decades of experience in running companies have enabled me to develop a process for driving startup success, including raising growth capital. When I formed my strategic advisory company, QuestFusion, to provide guidance to startups and growth companies, I began working with dozens of entrepreneurs on their business problems including strategy, product management, and raising capital. As a result of my experience and a broad-based need from startups and entrepreneurs, I codified a process to build successful companies and help them to raise growth capital for their businesses. This process is the **PLAN COMMIT WIN™ Methodology**, and it is designed to help you ascend the hierarchy of raising capital, and get to the top of the pyramid, while simultaneously getting the right investors into your company. The same process also dramatically improves your chances of business success, and improves your confidence and credibility with

> *Since these entrepreneurs do not have a way to diagnose the problem, they struggle to figure out how to fix it.*

Figure 1.1 - PLAN COMMIT WIN™ Methodology

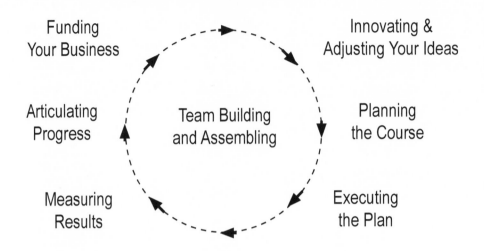

Funding Your Business

Innovating & Adjusting Your Ideas

Articulating Progress

Team Building and Assembling

Planning the Course

Measuring Results

Executing the Plan

outside investors. This is yet another reason why implementation of this process improves your chances of getting funded.

The **PLAN COMMIT WIN Methodology** is not a "pie in the sky" or theoretical approach to running businesses and raising capital. It is the same process that I have used to build successful businesses, raise over $200 million in equity capital for my companies, execute in over $2 billion in M&A transactions, and take a company from pre-product and pre-revenue to a successful IPO and eventually a $1 billion valuation. If you follow the steps of this process, it will significantly improve your chances for business success, and dramatically improve your chances of getting your company funded.

It takes about 90 days to implement the **PLAN COMMIT WIN Methodology** end-to-end, assuming you are starting from scratch. It can also be used as a screening process to see what components you may be missing from your process, plan or pitch. Successful companies eventually become profitable, or "self-funded," as we like to say in the startup world. But continuous implementation of the **PLAN COMMIT WIN Methodology** will continue to drive that success. Always keep in mind that the team is at the center of this process – and essential for all aspects of running a prosperous business. A key part of your team is your mentors and advisers.

Climbing the Pyramid: The Hierarchy of Raising Capital

The *PLAN COMMIT WIN Methodology* will allow you to climb the hierarchy of raising capital pyramid more quickly and efficiently, while removing many of the reasons and excuses for investors to say, "No thanks," or "We will pass." Raising money is like any sales process; you need to first remove the reason that people say no, then give them reasons to say yes. You have heard it before, and have no doubt experienced it yourself: people buy from people that they know, like and trust, and investors are no different. They want to find companies that have a compelling business model and a team that they trust, and that they believe can win.

This book will take you on the journey of ascending the hierarchy of raising outside capital through the application of the *PLAN COMMIT WIN Methodology*. Chapter 2, "It All Starts with an Idea," covers **smart ideation** and how to use innovation and adjustment to refine your idea. Chapter 3, "The Foundation of Any Good Plan," outlines the **strategic planning process** that is specifically designed for startup and growth companies. Chapters 4 through 7 describe the details of the strategic planning process and terminology, and tools that you will need to build a solid foundation for your business plan and business model. Specifically, Chapter 4, "Assessing the Landscape," goes into the contents of a **situation analysis** including markets, customers, competition, industry structure, the strengths & weaknesses of your company, and the resulting opportunities & threats. Chapter 5, "Available Provisions for the Journey," talks about your **financial goals** and how they tie to key milestones for your company. Chapter 6, "Focus on the Destination," walks through the process of the **winner's solution**, and how you describe total products and assess the scale of development projects. Chapter 7, "Necessary Resources to Succeed," looks at **gap analysis and gap resolution,** or the trade-offs between what you are trying to achieve in your winner's solution and the limits of your available financial resources. This becomes key later as you articulate why you need a specific amount of money in your funding request to investors. In Chapter 8, "Getting Specific about Your Plan," I outline the **annual operating plan, or AOP**, the budgeting process, and the contents of a fundable business plan. Some of the key elements about budgeting are also described in Chapter 5, "Available Provisions for the Journey," since it gives the basis for your budget from your financial goals in the strategic plan.

Chapter 9, "Building a Winning Team," talks about the entire process of **building and leading world-class teams** from scouting to recruiting to hiring to onboarding to leading and managing. Chapter 10, "Culture of Getting Things Done," discusses the importance of **execution**, and the critical nature of setting and meeting **key milestones**. This is a critical part of the process of building credibility with prospective investors. Finally, in Chapter 11, "Attracting the Right Investors," I discuss the **presentation and pitch deck**. I also outline the process for attracting and securing the right investors for your startup using a sales-funnel type process. With that background, let's look a little deeper, albeit still at a high level, at the application of the *PLAN COMMIT WIN Methodology* to climbing the pyramid.

Ideation

There are many sources of inspiration for business ideas, and **innovating and adjusting your idea** is at the heart of a startup. Ideas can come from your experience, how you look at the world and its problems, and how you formulate creative solutions. However, ideation is not just about the original "back of the envelope" or "bar room napkin" idea based on your initial observations. It is about refining that idea in the fire of the market – based on **customer feedback** – to make the idea into something worthwhile and valuable. It has to result in a product or service that is so valuable that customers are willing to pay more for it than it cost you to make. There also must be enough of those customers that you can make your idea into a successful business.

> *It (your idea) has to result in a product or service that is so valuable that customers are willing to pay more for it than it cost you to make.*

Strategic Planning

The first part of **planning the course** is setting the strategy. Therefore, the foundation of a good business plan requires a strategic planning process.

Startup leaders need to look "over the horizon" and "see the future" – and be able to focus within an instant on a critically important, very specific, short-term task. I call this **agility in vision**. It is the ability to go from a 30,000-foot view to a ground-level view, back up to 5,000 feet, and back down.

There is a scene in the Howard Hughes biography movie The Aviator where Leonardo DiCaprio – who plays Mr. Hughes – needs to make a decision about one of his most significant projects, the Hercules flying boat. He scans through his mind to gain focus on the task at hand while juggling all the other projects, big and small, in his vast empire of films, oil, aircraft, and airlines. Strategic planning requires that you undergo that kind of "mental scan" for your business. It is typically a forecast and projection of what you think will happen and how you want to react to the evolving business landscape over the planning cycle, which is typically three years. Since strategic planning is so critical and foundational to all higher levels of the pyramid, I have devoted five chapters to this topic.

Business Plan

This strategic plan will serve as the basis for your **AOP and budget**. This is the specific, month-by-month plan that you will use to manage your business and track key milestones and accomplishments. We will discuss the essential components of your AOP, and how you execute and track against it.

The next part of **planning the course** is to build your business plan. This is primarily a marketing document to help you raise capital for your company, so it's meant to **articulate progress** and your future plans. The business plan is based on the output of your strategic planning process and the specifics in your AOP. Once you have a business plan, you can develop the additional investor marketing tools, including an executive summary and an investor presentation.

Team

If you are building anything other than a sole proprietorship, you will clearly have other people involved in the company. To set yourself up for rapid growth and expansion, you will need a team.

You want to surround yourself with the best individuals you can get, and the best in their field, if possible. Because this is **your team**, you also want a group of people who work well together, and have a common set of goals and values to create the best possible culture.

So how do you identify people like that, and attract them to your company? Once you get those people on board, how do you make them as effective as possible in the shortest time? What are some of the key components of leading and coaching a stellar team? We will discuss all these things and more in the chapter on teams.

Execute

You will know your team is a winning one when you are able to **execute the plan** and deliver results. But – how do you know that you are doing those two things? You establish key deliverables and milestones, and **measure results** against your plan.

Organizations frequently overlook the importance of execution – and startups are no exception. It is essential to get things finished on time and on budget, while meeting all the customers' key requirements. If you make progress on your business plan and your business model makes sense, you will establish a track record with investors.

One of a startup's primary competitive advantages is speed of decision-making and focused execution. It is therefore a strategic imperative that a startup's leader not be paralyzed for fear of making the wrong decisions. You must have a bias towards action. Not everyone will agree with every decision you make. You will have to be comfortable with that. You need to drive alignment, even if you cannot get complete consensus.

Pitch

Once you have a solid business plan, a world-class team, a track record of execution, and specific milestones for your future, you will **articulate progress** and your future plan in order to attract the right investors to your company.

Although everyone's money is green, not every prospective investor can bring the right domain expertise, technical knowledge and experience to the table. Funding your business is not only about financial help – but also about gathering the right, smart people who can help propel your business forward. There are smart money investors who have domain expertise in your target vertical market. Bringing these people into the company becomes critically important when you are adding big investors who will become members of your board of directors.

The chapter on the Pitch and Presentation will discuss how to:

- Develop and learn to effectively use the executive summary, pitch deck, and business plan
- Create the investor funnel
- Give information to investors
- Create a compelling and clear investor pitch deck
- Learn how to deliver the pitch in a compelling way using stories
- Manage the investor sales funnel
- Create scarcity
- Negotiate term sheets
- Protect the interests of the founders, management team and employees
- Get the necessary capital from the right sources to help your company succeed

As mentioned in the introduction, this book is a step-by-step guide to help you establish a strong foundation for your business success and increase your chances of getting funded. The key components of this book are essential to running any small to midsize business or growth company.

So let's dive in.

CHAPTER 2

It All Starts with an Idea

Most ideas for businesses are bad. I do not say that to be mean; it is just true. Even some of the best business ideas started out as somewhat mediocre ideas. Even many **marginally** good ideas will not result in a successful business, because it is so difficult to disrupt the status quo and get customers to adopt something new from an unproved company. Poor business ideas are a big reason why so many startups fail. Throwing a lot of money at a bad business idea still will not make it succeed; it will just make it a **very expensive mistake.** I have seen this repeatedly in my career, including the 10 years that I spent in Silicon Valley – which is the center of gravity for venture capital, exceptional talent, startups, and innovative business ideas.

Figure 2.1 - Hierarchy for Raising Capital - Ideation

Sources for Business Ideas

There are an infinite number of ways to formulate new business ideas. I hunted around and found some common sources and uncovered a list in *Practical Business Ideas* that includes:

- Hobbies
- Experience
- The Media
- Exhibitions
- Surveys
- Complaints
- Brainstorming

This is a good list, and it drives home a point: the best business ideas are derived from your domain expertise and specialized knowledge. As an entrepreneur, you want to "mine" your experience for ideas, like prospectors mine for gold. A prospector can rarely find a valuable vein of gold with little or no work or effort. Entrepreneurship is similar.

Successful business people are typically very observant. They look at their world and ask:

- What problems exist out there?
- Do I have specialized knowledge that can help solve any of those problems?
- Do I have a hobby or some business experience that makes me uniquely qualified to propose credible solutions in this space?

You might find something in the media, a magazine, a newspaper, on TV, or on the web that resonates with your experience and hobbies. Can you provide special discernment that few others can? Maybe you have attended trade shows and exhibitions and seen things being made a certain way – that maybe you could make in a different, better and unique way.

Maybe you have conducted a survey or have received customer complaints where you work that identify other ways of doing something. Consistent customer problems are areas of opportunity. Brainstorm with colleagues or customers; they are good people to help you come up with ideas.

In the *PLAN COMMIT WIN Methodology*, we test the business validity of ideas from five distinct perspectives.

(1) The Customer Problem-Solution Test

The first test relates to the **value** of the idea. A good idea, from a business perspective, is one that **solves a real problem for a set of customers** in a big enough and rapidly growing market, with enough value in the solution that you can continue to grow your company over time. In short, you need a unique value proposition and a sustainable competitive advantage.

Assessing the idea from this perspective requires you to look at the customer problem that you are trying to solve. Before jumping right into your product or service, it is critically important to first dig deep into this issue. Entrepreneurs are frequently so eager to get going on their product that they do not take the time to develop an intimate understanding of the problem they are trying to solve – and the importance of having a solution for the target customers. These entrepreneurs may have a vague sense of the customers' pain points, but they do not always consider the nuances of the potential solutions from the target customers' perspective. You really need to dig deep and answer these questions:

- Is this an **important problem** for the customer?
- Is the customer **desperate** to solve this problem?
- Is **my idea vastly superior** to the alternative ways this problem is **currently** being addressed?

A winning idea solves **the biggest problem** that your prospective customers have – something they are losing sleep over. Additionally, they do not currently have a solution – or it is being solved in a much less efficient or cost-effective way. Ideally, your idea provides some innovation. In addition, that value proposition must be so superior to what is already in the market that customers are willing to take a risk on a startup company to deliver that solution.

Great entrepreneurs start with the problem they are trying to solve. Then, only after they develop a complete understanding of it, do they propose a unique and creative solution. The difference is both subtle and dramatic. If your idea does not have value to a customer – that is, if someone is not willing to pay for it – then you obviously cannot build a business around it. Your idea must have a **unique value proposition**, sometimes called a unique selling proposition, and solve an important customer problem.

I have attended dozens of investor meetings where an entrepreneur spends 90 percent of the time going on and on about their product and all the cool aspects of it – yet fails to discuss the details of the problem-solution, the value proposition, and the business model. Investors want to hear about your product, of course; but 80 percent of the meeting should cover the business model, and maybe 20 percent can focus on the product. I remind you of that ratio throughout the book, because it is so important.

(2) The Sustainable Competitive Advantage Test

The second test gauges your ability to **maintain a competitive position** over time. This is called a **sustainable competitive advantage**. Almost any idea can be copied or duplicated over time, with sufficient resources. For example, when people think of social networking, today they primarily think of Facebook.

There are other major players as well, including Instagram, which is owned by Facebook; LinkedIn, which is owned by Microsoft; YouTube and Google Plus, which are both owned by Google; Twitter, which is still independent; and most recently SnapChat, which recently went public. However, Friendster was founded in 2002, before the wider adoption of MySpace, Hi5, Facebook, and other social networking sites. Friendster was one of the first of these sites to attain over 1 million members, although several other smaller social networking sites preceded it. Despite Friendster's first-mover advantage, and first to get to reasonable scale, they are now dead. MySpace, which had a big lead on Facebook, is not dead, but it is a very niche solution. As you can see from this example, it is hard to create and maintain a competitive advantage.

Today's competitive advantage becomes the basis of competition over time. In other words, even if you have a feature or product that is different from what everyone else has, that difference will dissipate over time – and you will have to come up with something new. We will discuss that more in the chapter about the winner's solution. Getting back to Facebook, their ability to evolve and maintain a competitive advantage is what has made them so successful.

Good ideas for legitimate market opportunities will attract competition. Even if you are the first company to have a solution based on your idea, someone else will come up with a similar solution – eventually. If you are focused on a small niche market that does not offer much opportunity, you might not get competition; however, that also means that you are not catering to a potentially large and rapidly growing market opportunity.

It is essential that you understand your competitive advantage and how to sustain that advantage over time. If you have no competitive advantage, then your product or service is just a commodity – or even worse, it is worthless to potential customers.

(3) The Intersection Test

A great business idea occurs at the intersection of your domain knowledge, your passion, a unique value proposition for customers, a big market opportunity, and a team of passionate and focused people who can execute the plan.

I have found that the best ideas come from entrepreneurs with this magic combination of specialized knowledge, passion, and customer need.

If you have expertise without passion or momentum around it, it's nearly impossible to overcome the obstacles in your way. There is so much inertia from existing competition that you will not be able to break through. You need to have a deep-seated desire and belief that you are going to do something that is going to change the world in a positive way. You will gain from that as much as the clients and customers who are reaping the benefits. If you just have passion without some specialized knowledge or expertise, it usually just results in chaos, or best case, tons of energy with no focus. If there is no market or customer need, then there is no value proposition or viable business model.

Other important elements are finding a market that is potentially big and growing fast, and having a team that can deliver world-class execution. If there are only a handful of small customers for a product or service, it isn't really that interesting as a fundable business proposition.

(4) The Market Size and Growth Test

It is critical to point out that a good business idea, from a venture capital perspective, must address a potentially large – specifically, a multi-billion dollar – market with explosive growth potential. If a company is addressing a rapidly growing market opportunity, once it has revenue, it is typically at least doubling in revenue every year for three to five years, and sometimes longer. For example, the 2017 eligibility requirements for consideration in the *Deloitte Fast 500* include being in business for a minimum of four years, having fiscal year 2013 operating revenues of at least $50,000 USD, and fiscal year 2016 operating revenues of at least $5 million USD with a growth rate of 75 percent or greater.

Why is growth so important? In the *McKinsey & Co.* article, "Grow Fast or Die Slow," they state that there are three things that make growth the most important factor for business success. First, growth yields greater returns. High-growth companies offer a return to shareholders five times greater than medium-growth companies. Second, growth predicts long-term success. "Supergrowers" – companies whose growth was greater than 60 percent when they reached $100 million in revenues – were eight times more likely to reach $1 billion in revenues than those growing less than 20 percent. Additionally, growth matters more than margin or cost structure.

Increases in revenue growth rates drive twice as much market-capitalization gain as margin improvements for companies with less than $4 billion in revenues. Size and growth are paramount when you are seeking outside investment for your startup.

(5) The Idea Refinement Test

Now let's talk a little bit about idea refinement. Maybe your idea is a diamond in the rough. How do you make sure that this concept is one that really resonates with customers? You must **refine your idea**, the same way that crude oil is refined into valuable and usable fuels.

This is when having a technical advisory board and a business advisory board becomes instrumental. Industry insiders with domain and technical experience in your vertical markets can be excellent "sounding boards," and their feedback is essential. When you are seeking advisory board members, look for people who are willing to ask difficult questions, play "Devil's advocate," and do not have any conflicts of interest. Work with your corporate attorney when establishing advisory boards, since they can help you establish the terms for members.

The second thing you need to do to refine your idea is to get opinions from expert sources in the market. As such, you need "teaching customers" that will share insights with you. Not all customers will have the patience and willingness to give you feedback and guidance. You will have to seek them out and cultivate them. The two most important ways to get comments from customers is by giving something to get something, or quid pro quo, and listening. I cannot tell you the number of times that people either do not ask questions, or they do not listen to the response that customers provide. In a business to business, or B2B setting, you should build close personal relationships with key decision-makers at your customer. Build relationships with everyone, even the executive assistants. Focus on helping them achieve their goals. In this way, you have a better chance of building "teaching customer" relationships. You should build relationships, even in times of difficulty. As Bill Gates said, "Your most unhappy customers are your greatest source of learning." After you have talked with your advisers and have some comments from experts in your target market, you can do broader target customer surveys. I talk more about market research in the next chapter.

Ultimately, you will likely need to make incremental refinements and improvements to your idea until it gets to the point where it has a lot of value. It does not need to be perfect; it just needs to be better than everything else that's out there, and solve a real problem for the customer. Ideally your solution is at least 10x better in terms of price-performance versus alternatives. This means either 10 times cheaper, or 10 times better, or some combination of the two. You might keep making incremental refinements over time to have a sustainable competitive advantage, but getting a "good enough" product into real customers' hands sooner is infinitely better than getting a "perfect" product into their hands too late. Include the features you want to add in the future in your product roadmap.

The companies I have seen do a great job solving problems in this environment build trust and credibility with customers. You should always get back to your customers in a timely fashion, solve their problems quickly, and consistently provide superior price-performance. All of these things build upon themselves and give you a stronger position to maintain your brand over time. You never want to **create** problems for the sake of solving them, of course; but you need to rise to the occasion when they surface.

If you are in an industry or field where you can develop prototypes, it's worth doing that. Many of my prior companies were semiconductor chip businesses, and it's hard to prototype chips – but we could do system-level prototypes that we used for demonstrations and simulations. It is always best to show customers what you are doing and how the solution works, and get direct feedback around those experiences. This type of feedback can be invaluable and save enormous amounts of time and money.

An effective entrepreneurial process consists of listening to customers, refining your idea and roadmap over time, and iterating as you go. This ensures that your business idea is viable, has value for customers, and that you are sustaining your competitive advantage over time.

A new buzzword being circulated widely in the startup community – and one that I first mentioned in the book's Introduction – is "pivot." Very few companies succeed with their original idea without making **any** changes or refinements. In some cases, the change in direction may be more abrupt, and is called a "pivot." Establishing a response loop based on interaction with customers in your target market will help you to refine your idea, and thus make it even more valuable. You need to be willing to adjust your market direction and focus. At the same time, if you constantly pivot, you will never make progress in any direction. Startups that pivot one or two times raise 2.5x more money, have 3.6x better user growth, and are 52 percent less likely to scale prematurely than startups that pivot more than two times or not at all. You need to be very thoughtful and deliberate when you make a significant change in your product or market focus – and be sure that it's a change worth making.

Case Study: Product Centric View versus a Customer Problem-Solution Focus

I worked on a product at my former company, Entropic, that enabled multi-room DVR. To do this, the solution needed to stream up to six channels of high quality HDTV video room-to-room in a house. Each channel needed to have full DVR capabilities including record, fast forward, rewind and pause. There were other home networking technologies, like Wi-Fi, that were good for data networking in the home; however, they did not solve the unique set of problems associated with streaming multiple video channels to all the TVs in the home. Entropic therefore developed a product and associate system solution technology that solved the "whole home streaming problem" by using the coaxial cable TV cables already installed in the home.

Because there were huge technical challenges to get this to work, it was difficult for others to duplicate. It required an understanding of communications system engineering, software, and various semiconductor technology disciplines to develop a product. Even after we developed a working prototype, we still needed to do lot of work to prove the technology functioned properly.

The product-centric view of the technology included the need to work on the cable TV infrastructure already installed in the home. Homes with more than one TV set – which is required for multi-room DVR – have "splitters" in the home that take one cable and split it into two or more outputs. These splitters are designed to **isolate** rooms from each other, so in order to communicate room-to-room, you have to overcome this technical challenge.

Another challenge is a communication system phenomenon called multi-path. Think about yelling into the mountains and getting an echo. In a communication system, you need to distinguish between the original signal (your voice) and a multi-path signal (the echo). In the case of the in-home cable TV cables, the echo can be as loud as the original signal, so it is tough to distinguish between the two signals. In some cases, there can be multiple echoes, which makes the challenge even tougher.

I wrote the above paragraph to talk specifically about the product instead of the solution or the "killer app" that the solution enables. I made a major effort to try to describe the technical aspects of the product more or less in layman's terms – and it is still very technically complex. Did reading that make your head hurt? At the very least did you have to go over it a few times to understand what I was saying? It is not easy to follow very technical things, even if you concentrate, unless you are a technical specialist in that field.

This is what a prospective investor hears when an entrepreneur presents the story about his or her company from a technology and product-centric point of view. Instead, focus on the customer problem and the benefits of your solution! Put things into layman's terms, or language that can be easily understood by your audience. For example: Our technology enables DVR functionality at every TV in the house with a single DVR and a client set-top box at the other TVs. We support full DVR capability at each TV, and our solution lowers the cost of implementing this capability by over $200 in the average US TV home. This is an extremely difficult technical challenge and we have over 15 patents related to this technology.

To ensure widespread adoption of the technology, Entropic also established an industry alliance called the Multimedia over Coax Alliance (MoCA), pronounced "Mo-Kah," like the tasty chocolate coffee beverage. The alliance was composed of ecosystem partners, like Pay TV service providers including EchoStar/Dish Network, Cox Communications, Time Warner Cable, Comcast, and Verizon, as well as equipment manufacturers like Motorola and Cisco, and eventually potential competitors like Broadcom. Entropic, and eventually the alliance, conducted extensive field trials to prove the viability and reliability of the technology. Even then, we had to do a lot of work selling the value proposition to our potential customers and our customers' customers. All of these established barriers to entry and built switching costs – both of which help to sustain a competitive advantage.

Although MoCA became a written and documented standard, the standard did not specify how to implement the solution – which was an additional barrier to entry. MoCA became the de facto industry standard for home networking of digital entertainment, was in over 50 percent of US TV homes by the end of 2014 and had gained widespread deployment in several other countries around the globe.

Over the next several years, Entropic executed on a roadmap with higher performance versions of MoCA, which also helped to sustain a competitive advantage. The product roadmap included enhanced performance, higher levels of integration, greater robustness, and other features that we found customers desired as they started using the product in their systems.

Interestingly, the value proposition for MoCA was different at different parts of the supply chain. In other words the value to the consumer was different from the Pay TV service provider, which was different from our direct customers, the set-top box OEMs. So, we had to describe the solution in different ways to different constituencies. And in order to be effective, we had to do it in a language that each constituency would clearly understand. When describing the problem and solution to prospective investors, we had to use other analogies and stories to explain the value proposition and market opportunity.

In summary, we had to have a unique value proposition that worked along all parts of the value chain, and we needed to articulate it in a way that each different target audience would understand. This is something to keep in mind as you develop your own solutions.

Guidance From a "Teaching Customer"

Several years ago, I was working for a company called C-Cube Microsystems that provided the enabling technology for making DVD players and digital set-top boxes. In November of 1998 I received an urgent call the day before Thanksgiving from Usui-san, the then-president of C-Cube Japan. Usui-san had received a call from Tanaka-san, a high level General Manager at JVC – one of our largest customers for DVD processing chips, and a very important "teaching customer" who had helped us navigate through many nuances of implementing our DVD chip and software technologies into actual products.

JVC was having significant issues with one of our products, and was in jeopardy of missing a critical product launch if we could not solve the problems right away. The conversation went something like this:

Usui-san: JVC needs to see you.
Me: When?
Usui-san: Now.
Me: Why do they need to see me?
Usui-san: They remember you are in charge of all DVD products.
Me: Can they wait a week?
Usui-san: No. They need to see you now.

This was Usui-san's uniquely subtle way of saying, "The customer is ready to kick us out of the account and we will never do business with them again unless you do what they ask RIGHT NOW!" So I let my wife know I was going to have to miss Thanksgiving to go to Japan.

Usui-san was the meeting facilitator. Our Japanese sales engineer and field applications engineer both had a good sense of the issues, and gave me a thorough briefing prior to the customer meeting. As a result of the customer meeting, we established a "Tiger Team" – with members from the C-Cube headquarters, C-Cube Japan, and JVC – based on the feedback we got from this teaching customer. As a result, we were able to identify some key limitations of our solution in the customer's application.

This team was able to brainstorm and come up with some great ideas and potential solutions. We established a plan with key milestones that were based on the JVC launch timing and priorities of which features were "must have" versus "like to have." The clearly defined milestones galvanized the team and kept them focused on key activities. The deadlines provided us with early warning signals if we weren't keeping on schedule, which then allowed management to deploy more resources in areas where they were needed most.

We maintained an ongoing dialogue between the customer, the field engineering team, and the factory engineering team. The "Tiger Team" held a daily conference call and kept me in the loop with key updates and issues, so Usui-san could keep senior management at JVC informed, and ensure alignment with what they heard from their own team. They kept me abreast of all "big picture" activities, so that I would be aware if I needed to jump in at any point.

We were able to deploy the product with JVC and drive revenue. This teaching customer's tough love and commitment to us taught us a number of critical things that were not proprietary to JVC. They helped raise our awareness about items that needed to be in our DVD solutions for robustness in a variety of applications of the product. This allowed us to drive significant revenue in the broader market. JVC remained one of C-Cube's most loyal customers during my entire tenure at the company – and Tanaka-san remained a good friend and advocate of C-Cube.

As an entrepreneur, you need to be prepared to do whatever it takes – within ethical boundaries, of course – to serve the customer... even if it means missing Thanksgiving dinner. If you can have a culture like that, and drive a process to resolve problems and build trust, you have a great chance of making your idea into a great business idea – and ultimately building a successful company.

CHAPTER 3

The Foundation of any Good Plan

An investor is not likely to ask you, "Did you run a strategic planning process?" So why is this a critical building block to getting funding? It is because investors expect you to have an in-depth understanding of your target market, customer, and the current and potential competitive landscape for your products. They expect to see a financial plan that is based on something more than your best guess or what you hope will happen. They expect you to fully understand your business model and financial projections, and be able to justify that model. They expect you to be able to clearly articulate your unique value proposition and sustainable competitive advantage. They want to know that your target market is potentially large and growing very fast in a quantitative way. They want to understand your assumptions, and judge whether they are reasonable and viable. Investors want to know that you are the right leader and that you have the right team to make your business a success.

Figure 2.1 - Hierarchy for Raising Capital - Strategic Planning

The **PLAN COMMIT WIN *Methodology*** provides a very systematic way of obtaining all the critical data that investors seek from startup companies looking to raise outside capital.

What is a Strategic Planning Process?

Like any process, a strategic planning process has a clearly defined set of steps and specific outcomes. It requires that you look at your market, customer, competitive landscape, and industry structure; as well as company strengths, weaknesses, opportunities and threats. I recommend that you do this for a three-year forecast period. This time horizon is usually good for startups, since it helps you plan a product and business strategy that drives optimal success for your company. Some investors may want a five-year forecast for doing their own financial models. If this is the case, you can extrapolate years four and five from year three. A well-run strategic planning process allows you to align your team and other company stakeholders around a common set of goals and objectives, and it gives a common context for communication and discussion of key elements of your business success. It also grounds your vision into an actionable plan.

Startups are a special breed of company with a significant amount of uncertainty and risk. Many a startup CEO uses this ambiguity as an excuse to avoid planning – which is just a recipe for disaster. After running and working with many startups, the strategic planning process I have developed is particularly well suited for startups and small businesses. I outline this process in the next few chapters, and provide some illustrative examples, worksheets, and checklists that will help you navigate through it.

If you are in the "ideation" stage of a startup company, you will use the tools I have provided in a different way. You will really want to focus on the validation of your market opportunity and target customer, as we discussed in the prior chapter. Since you do not yet have an actual product or customer, you want to develop a clear description of the problem you are trying to solve, and how this solution is unique and highly valuable to your target customers. You must then test these assumptions in a cost-effective way. If you are at this stage, it is unlikely that you will be seeking institutional financing for your venture. If you are at this pre-seed stage from a financing perspective, you typically must rely upon bootstrapping – that is, using your own money – or relying on help from friends and family.

If you have sufficient validation of your business model, you may be ready for Seed Stage investment, which typically comes from Angel investors. The best Angels to seek out in this situation are those with domain expertise and technical knowledge in your target product-market segment. You will still need to have some level of strategic planning and market analysis when talking with this class of investors; however, it is less rigorous than if you are seeking Series A or growth stage financing from venture capital.

As you get your first customer and validate your idea, you will gather more data and do a better job of planning and forecasting. A strategic planning process will allow you to look at things in a systematic way – one that brings you and your team out of the day-to-day tactics of running the business to focus on ways to build long-term growth and value for your company.

There are a number of other reasons for running a strategic planning process for your startup or small business:

- It ensures that your company's vision and mission are grounded in a strong plan of action.
- It allows you to critically assess your market focus and align it with the best growth opportunities for the company.
- It aids in identifying areas where your company needs to build core competencies, or shore up your existing core competencies.
- It helps to identify areas for strategic partnerships, and a partner ecosystem that can be critically important to execute your overall vision.
- It allows you to assess your financing requirements over the next few years.
- It serves as a starting point for a good annual operating plan and a budgeting process.
- It is the foundation for a business plan that you would use to raise money for your company.

Often when you are caught up in daily business, you think, "I do not have time to run a strategic planning process. I'm too busy running my business." Running a startup is tough. There is never enough time or resources to do everything that you want to do, and there is always pressure to accomplish a lot in a very short time.

However, as Benjamin Franklin said, "By failing to prepare, you are preparing to fail." Planning is an essential part of building a successful business. As Michael Porter, the famous Harvard professor who focuses on business strategy, explains, "Strategy is about making choices and trade-offs. It's about deliberately choosing to be different." A strategic planning process is essential for business success and for raising the required growth capital that you need to fuel your company. Finally, you need to make sure your plan is grounded in action and execution.

Strategic Planning is Critical for
Raising Outside Investment for a Startup

One of the primary focuses of a CEO – in addition to running the company – is raising money. As I mentioned in Chapter 1, the one thing startup CEOs lose the most sleep over is getting their next round of financing. Even if you are a solopreneur or small-to-midsize business owner, it is important to understand the capital requirements of your business that you need to establish your venture and fuel your growth.

Money is the "fuel in the gas tank" that allows you to "run the engine" of your business. When I was a startup CEO, I would spend between 20 and 40 percent of my time in the early and growth stages of our company on investor relations activities. These activities typically include attending investor conferences and holding small group and one-on-one meetings with current and prospective investors in your company. Even when you are not actively raising capital, you must still spend time cultivating potential investors for future rounds of financing. You are always building your credibility, relationships and track record.

After I took Entropic public, investor relations were still a key part of running the company. It continued to be important to cultivate and inform investors and analysts to help drive visibility and increase the company stock price. In rare circumstances, I have seen a company's Chief Financial Officer take a lead role in this investor relations activity. But even in those cases, the CEO needs to actively engage with current and potential investors.

With all the time and effort required to run the company and raise money, when are you supposed to plan? The answer is that you have to make time for planning and other strategic activities. The vast majority of entrepreneurs have never run a detailed and thorough strategic planning process. I know this because I meet with them every day, and they do not have the answers to basic questions about their business – questions that could be answered as a result of running such a process. This includes answers to basic questions like:

- Who is your customer?
- What problem are you solving for them?
- What makes your solution unique?
- Who is your competition?

- What is your competitive advantage?
- How big is your market?
- How fast is it growing?
- What is your business model?

Honestly, it is shocking. Don't be that entrepreneur! Implement the principles in this book!

Establishing a Foundation for Raising Outside Capital

Let's revisit the Hierarchy of Raising Capital. Your goal is to get the money at the top of the pyramid – and there is a defined set of steps that you must take to ascend it. These are the building blocks you must put in place to successfully raise outside capital for your company. If you complete these foundational activities, you will massively increase your chances of raising money from the right investors.

At the base of that pyramid is ideation, which we covered in the last chapter. Next is the strategic planning process, which we cover in the next few chapters. The output of the strategic planning process is the natural starting point for developing an annual operating plan, a budget, and a business plan that you can share with investors. It's hard to have an investor presentation – much less an intelligent investor conversation – without a reasonable business plan. You also need the business plan to come up with a decent executive summary, and a well-thought-out funding request. These are the tools you need to get your company funded.

Investors also need to believe that you and your team can execute the plan. In order to establish credibility with investors, you need to set and meet key milestones. This will help you create a track record and credibility. The process of raising capital from Angel investors or venture capitalists is typically a multi-month process. It takes, on average, three to six months to raise a round of financing. At the beginning of this process, you should show milestones that you expect to meet during the fundraising process. As you have follow-up meetings with investors, you can show your progress by citing achievement of these milestones. Prospective investors in your company will ask themselves, "Is this a team that can execute this plan?" Part of a solid strategic planning process is defining your critical core competencies, and having a plan to build a team with expertise in those areas. You have a current team, and you need to have a plan to build a world-class team that can execute your plan.

Once you have completed these steps, you can begin to develop an investor presentation that has the content and depth necessary for raising outside capital. This includes the pitch deck itself, but also how you present and your credibility with investors. Following these steps will significantly improve your chances of raising money and the amounts of money you need to fuel your growth strategy. You are also more likely to get the right investors into your deal at a suitable valuation.

The Strategic Planning Process

I have tried dozens of tools in the process of strategic, business, and product planning throughout my career. The process I have outlined in this book only includes approaches that I have found to work in startups and growth stage companies. If you do not currently plan, even using a subset of these tools can dramatically improve your decision-making, chances of success, ability to communicate your story, and chances of getting funded.

The Strategic Planning Process for Startups that we use in the *PLAN*

Figure 3.2 - Strategic Planning Process

COMMIT WIN Methodology starts with a **Situation Analysis**. This is just a map of the target market landscape and where you are today. The first step is to look at your **overall market** size and potential growth, and answer these four questions:

- What **focus market** are you going after? Be as specific as you can.
- How **large** is it?
- What is the size of the **total available market** and the **served available market**?
- How much **market share** can you realistically carve out with your solution?

Next, you need to learn as much as you can about your target customers' needs, problems, and desires. What are the problems that you are trying to solve for them, and how are you doing that in a unique way versus your competition?

Next, consider your **competition and potential competition**. How do your product's features stack up against direct competitors, substitutes, and potential new entrants to the market? How entrenched is the competition and potential competition with the customers at a company level? You need to be able to answer all these questions if you are going to displace an entrenched incumbent in your industry.

When we were developing and first commercializing the MoCA solution at Entropic, we had no MoCA competition since we invented the technology. However, we knew that if MoCA was successful, Broadcom – a key supplier of communications technologies to our target customers – would eventually buy Entropic or develop their own MoCA solutions.

If someone already has a solution – or if you are going after an existing solution with a totally novel approach – what are the existing competitors going to do as a reaction to you coming into the market?

Industry Structure Analysis, also known as Porter's Five Forces Analysis, is a very useful tool in assessing the current situation. It's based on the observation that profit margins vary between industries, which can be explained by the structure of an industry. Although the concept of industry structure analysis has been around for a long time, Michael Porter popularized a model in his book Competitive Strategy that can be very useful for strategic planning.

One highly valuable tool for assessing both competition and your company in general is a company strengths, weaknesses, opportunities and threats, or **SWOT Analysis**. It is critically important to be honest when conducting a SWOT, or it will be worth squat.

Financial Goals focus on the financial resources you have at your disposal, and what financial milestones you can expect to accomplish as a result of that investment. Next you look at the **Winner's Solution** – where you ultimately want to go over the next three years, with one, two and three-year milestones. This helps you develop a product roadmap that allows your company to maintain a sustainable competitive advantage over time. You also need to consider the ecosystem you need, and build it around your product or service to make it successful.

The next step is to do a **Gap Analysis**. This asks: What is the distance from Point A to Point B – from the Situation Analysis to your Winner's Solution – under the constraints of your Financial Goals? You then create a **Gap Resolution** for each of the major gaps. Some gaps may also exist in your organization and product plans. Finally, that flows naturally into having a **Strategic Plan** that will be the guideline for your company over the next three years.

Keep in mind when building a business that you want to solve problems that have a long life and solutions that can adapt to changing market requirements. This is an important reason to do strategic planning. It does not need to be a bureaucratic and cumbersome planning process that takes several months to complete – or one where your solution is obsolete by the time you finish. Market dynamics change too rapidly in startup-land for such an approach. The plan outlined above is a more streamlined process that has worked for the startups and growth stage companies I have run. The reasoning that "things are changing too fast" is not an excuse to skip planning. Develop a plan, execute and adjust.

Strategic Planning is Like "Going to the Mall" or "Taking a Nature Hike"

When you go shopping, you (usually) want to leave the store with what you wanted to buy – and nothing else. When you go on a hike, you want to walk out of the woods still alive, healthy, and happy. You do not want to spend money on many impulse purchases or die in the woods. Implicit in each of these things is a goal – and you improve your chances of achieving that goal dramatically if you have a plan. As Yogi Berra said, "If you don't know where you're going, you'll end up someplace else."

You can think of the situation analysis as a topographical map of your company, in the context of the market, customer, competitors, potential competitors, and other industry structural issues. You know those big maps at the shopping mall? Before you look for where you want to go, you walk up to it initially to get your bearings. You look for the big red dot that says "**You Are Here**." In short, you need to know where you are, and where you want to go. In creating and growing a business, you want to have a map of what the landscape looks like in your marketplace, and how it is likely to evolve over time. Situation analysis gives you a map and tells you where you are. The winner's solution is where you want to go. Since there are not unlimited resources available to a startup – or to any company for that matter – you need to have a set of financial goals and constraints.

If you are going on a hike or about to climb a mountain, you need to know the distance and terrain from Point A to Point B. This is where gap analysis and resolution come into play – and the point at which you need to ask yourself:

- What are your critical milestones over the next four to six quarters?
- What key skills will you need to have on your team to accomplish these milestones?
- What are some of the likely obstacles you will face in the next 12 to 18 months?
- How much money do you need to accomplish your goals?
- What other resources will you need?
- How will you use the money?
- What are the key things you are monitoring in your market and the competitive landscape?

Before you go on a hike, you make a list of things to pack. In much the same way, you need the proper resources and provisions in business to get from Point A to Point B. In the strategic plan, Point A is your situational analysis and Point B is your winner's solution.

On very difficult and long hikes, you may need a guide. If you climb Mt. Everest and you want to come back alive, you need a Sherpa – a guide who has experience in the process of climbing that mountain.

Several years ago, I went helicopter skiing in the Bugaboos in British Columbia, Canada. A significant amount of the skiing is "sub-Alpine," which basically means skiing in the forest with trees all around you. Skiers need to avoid "tree wells" – huge ditches that form around the base of trees when it snows, that can be more than 30 feet deep. Needless to say, this is vastly different from skiing at a more traditional ski resort. There is also a reasonable risk of avalanches in the Alpine skiing areas of heli-skiing. As such, the first full day at Canadian Mountain Holidays, or CMH, is dedicated to safety and how to find any fellow skiers that are buried in the snow by an avalanche. My advice: Do not go heli-skiing without an experienced guide. The CMH guides are not only expert skiers; they are experts in knowing the mountains where you are skiing. They usually assign two guides per group with one in the front and one in the back. You want to have fun, and you need to avoid stupid mistakes.

Business is no different. As an entrepreneur, you should get a coach or mentor to be your guide along the way. If you have a good mentor, you will be more efficient, more effective, more successful, and have more fun.

Finally, the outcomes of a strategic planning process are your product roadmaps; resource plan; rough headcount requirements; core competencies that you have and need to build; strategic alliances you already have and those you need to put in place; a set of intermediate milestones; and the ultimate results that you are trying to achieve over the next three years.

> *As an entrepreneur, you should get a coach or mentor to be your guide along the way.*

Although the plan will have some annual milestones, you should have more frequent milestones for the first 18 months. Your strategic plan naturally leads into the next step of planning: creating an annual operating plan, or AOP, including a monthly budget. Any company that takes outside capital is going to be judged on these kinds of metrics. Without the foundation of a strategic plan, it's much more difficult – if not impossible – to put together an annual operating plan and a budget that makes sense. This level of basic planning is necessary for creating a business plan that will withstand outside investors' scrutiny and increase your chances of success. Over the next four chapters, we dive deeper into the detailed steps of the strategic planning process.

CHAPTER 4

Assessing the Landscape

The Situation Analysis of your strategic plan is essential for your annual operating plan, business plan, and investor presentation. You will be lost without a map of your market landscape – and even if you do not feel lost, prospective investors will. You need to know your current "coordinates" – from a market, customer, competitive, and industry structure standpoint – before you can realistically establish a set of achievable future objectives and plot a course to accomplish these goals.

A situation analysis answers these key questions:

- What is the size and growth of your target market?
- What does your customer "look like"?
- Why is your offering important and relevant to your customer?

- Is what you offer critically important to your customer over the long term?
- How do you stack up against the competition?
- What are the key elements of your industry structure?
- How does your business make money?
- What are your key strengths and weaknesses?
- What are you doing to build upon your strengths and mitigate your weaknesses?
- What are the primary opportunities and threats?
- What are your plans to capitalize on key opportunities?
- What are your plans to mitigate significant threats?

Figure 4.1 - Strategic Planning Process - Situation Analysis

The situation analysis portion draws a topographical map that allows you to navigate the rest of the strategic planning process. Once you know "where you are" relative to your ecosystem, you can establish "where you want to go" and in what timeframe. Knowing your ultimate goal from a total product standpoint and product roadmap – which we will discuss in Chapter 6 on the winner's solution – is an essential part of knowing where you want to go. You also want to establish your business model, build your company for long-term success, and achieve your financial goals. As an investor, I see too many entrepreneurs beaming with confidence and enthusiasm with a "strategy" that is based on nothing more than hope and wishful thinking. As they say, "Hope is not a strategy."

Figure 4.2 - Strategic Analysis Key Components

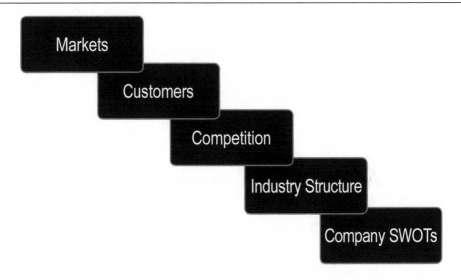

What is a Target Market?

The first part of a market analysis is defining your target market. A market is simply a collection of customers that have a common set of needs and buying behavior. The first step is to determine the common customer problem that you are looking forward to solving. This will be the vertical market that you want to attack.

Let's look at a ridiculous example of poor target marketing:

Investor says to the entrepreneur: "Who are the customers for your product?"

Entrepreneur says: "Everyone could use this product, so my market is all consumers."

Investor says: "That's interesting. What's your marketing strategy?"

(While thinking, This person is an idiot, but I really want to hear what they say.)

Entrepreneur says: "The internet. My website and social media channels."

This might seem like a ridiculous situation, and it's clearly not a very well-thought-out plan; but you would be surprised by how many times I have had conversations not too far from this. Don't be that entrepreneur!

When you define your target market, you will begin to understand the opportunity for your solution. How big of a niche do you want to go after? This is a relatively simple question, but the answer can be quite complex. You need to consider things like the scalability of your solution, the number of customers, and those customers' buying habits. You need to clearly define what that target market looks like, how you will reach that market (i.e., your sales channels), and the value of your solution for this group.

It is best to define a defensible niche that you can dominate that has the potential to lead to a massive and rapidly growing market. Most investors are reluctant to invest in companies that want to "boil the ocean," which is a term for going after an extremely broad horizontal market. "Everyone" is not a target. In fact, it is the opposite of a target. Intelligent investors will get up and run if you tell them that your success strategy is based on just getting two or three percent of a massive market. Even if they physically do not run just to be polite, they have mentally left the building.

> *It is best to define a defensible niche that you can dominate that has the potential to lead to a massive and rapidly growing market.*

Targeted marketing is the intersection of your product with a specific set of customers who have a clear need for a solution to an important problem for them. Your product solves that problem in a unique way that is very valuable to the customers. No matter what you are selling, your solution needs to fulfill an unmet need or desire of the target customers. Even in the case where you are selling video games, you are fulfilling a need for the customer to be entertained or bond with their friends or other online gamers. This gets to product-market segmentation.

The best business opportunities – and thus, the best investment opportunities – have been with companies who offer a differentiated solution that has great value to a set of customers in a target market that's potentially very large and has the potential to experience explosive growth.

Some would say, "What about Facebook and Amazon? They address massive horizontal markets, don't they?" Let's take a look at both of these examples. Facebook started as an online social network for university students. In fact, you could not even get on Facebook in the early days if you did not have a ".edu" email address. That is the essence of target marketing. What about Amazon, the world's largest online retailer? Amazon initially focused just on books. They did not enter other product sales online until they had established an extremely strong position in books. That is target marketing.

Of course the trick to finding a great startup business is to identify these emerging market opportunities early, before anyone else spots them or has a solution in the works. You then need to develop a creative solution with a unique value proposition and a sustainable competitive advantage. Alternatively, you can be a fast follower with a superior solution to the first mover, a better intellectual property position, a superior cost structure, and better team to execute the strategy. However, these fast follower deals are very hard to get funded unless the first mover really does not have much of a lead, or you have a team with a proven track record with the venture capital community.

Once you have defined your target market, you can then forecast that market's size and growth – as well as your estimated market share. You need to clearly state your assumptions. Investors are likely to challenge some of your assumptions. You need to listen with an open mind, especially if the challenge has merit. If you still feel strongly about an assumption, you need to be ready to defend it…without appearing defensive!

Key Elements of Market Analysis

In order to understand market analysis, let's look at some basic definitions in the context of strategic planning:

Total Available Market (TAM): Total size of the market including all substitute products and adjacent products in your target market.

Served Available Market (SAM): Size of the market including your direct competitors – a subset of the TAM.

Market Growth: The single-year or multi-year revenue growth of a market opportunity, usually expressed as a Compounded Annual Growth Rate, or CAGR, as a percentage.

Market Share: Your Company's percentage of the SAM. You can look at this for revenue and units. It is instructive to look at it both ways, but the most important is revenue.

Ultimately, you want to size the market by looking at both the total available market and the served available market size over three years. This can be difficult in the startup world, since you are frequently going after a market that does not currently exist. However, if you look a little deeper, you can usually see a current market that you are trying to replace, or a set of emerging factors that will allow your market to emerge and grow. This is not to say that there are no breakthrough innovations in markets that previously did not exist. A classic example of this is Mosaic, the first popular web browser, invented by Marc Andreessen and Eric Bena at the University of Illinois, which greatly helped spread knowledge and usage of the World Wide Web. This type of innovation is what Peter Thiel is talking about in his book, *Zero to One*.

Identifying Emerging Markets

As an entrepreneur, you are likely something of a trailblazer. Blazing a trail is different than hiking on an already established trail, and vastly different from driving on a paved road. You need to identify the best route to get you to the key points of interest while remaining safe. If you are a smart trailblazer, you will look to create a path with the least amount of effort needed.

Entrepreneurs are also like farmers. Smart farmers want to plant their crops on fertile ground; but if they do not have a massive bankroll, they will need to find the best piece of land with the least amount of rocks and stones, and soil that has the right characteristics for growing. If you are getting a field ready to grow crops, you have to get that field ready quickly and start growing. Your crops will grow faster and healthier, and yield greater results on fertile ground.

Smart entrepreneurs want to find the best path to deliver the maximum results with the least amount of effort. This requires that they identify markets that are ripe for growth – and often see a ripeness that's not apparent to the casual observer, except in hindsight of course. In emerging markets it is important to be a little early, and never be late.

The best way to identify these markets is by looking at the broader ecosystem. For example, when Henry Ford introduced the assembly line for mass production of automobiles, people could use them because roads were already built to support a horse and carriage. In fact, early automobiles were called horse-less carriages. A more recent example of infrastructure being already in place is Uber. Before Uber, there was widespread use of mobile phones with Global Positioning System, or GPS technology for location services. There were a number of underutilized limo drivers that had an excess capacity. Without that, Uber could not have been successful.

"Tops-Down" Market Modeling

Developing a so-called "tops-down" market model that supports your revenue projections will add significant credibility to your forecasts. The best way to do this is to leverage the "infrastructure" data that your company's emerging market is reliant upon, and extrapolate the market size from this data. This approach is based on the idea of solving a key customer problem and replacement of an inferior substitute product based upon innovation that has a superior price-performance. It simply will not be possible to get direct market data in some emerging markets; even when it's available, it is usually wrong. This is where you need to be creative in deriving a SAM from available TAM data for markets that are related or derivative to your target market. Getting supportive feedback from key lead customers that validates some of your assumptions can be invaluable for adding credibility to your story.

Change Factors Analysis

An extremely useful tool for looking at market dynamics is called the Change Factors Matrix – sometimes called a PESTEL Analysis. PESTEL models are frequently used just to look at the external Political, Economic, Social, Technological, Environmental, and Legal factors affecting your market and company. However, it is just as important to look at the internal aspects of what your company can do proactively to impact factors in these areas.

Table 4.1 - Change Factors Analysis

	External	Internal
Political		
Economic		
Social		
Technological		
Environmental		
Legal		

To forecast market growth, you need to understand market dynamics. What external environmental factors are going to have an impact on the market size and growth? What is the overall market opportunity? What internal things can you do that will help to accelerate the market opportunity? Is there an initial opportunity in a protected niche where you can dominate before launching the product in a broader market? In other words, how big a slice can you carve out of the TAM with your solution – and over what timeframe? The "slice" that is directly available to your solution and your direct competitors is by definition your SAM.

For example, government regulation and deregulation can both create opportunities and threats. External factors are elements outside of your control that you need to be prepared to address. All too often, companies consider macroeconomics and political factors as critical external factors.

However, there are usually a number of external factors that have a more direct relationship to your market opportunity.

Examples of political factors that could directly relate to your business include specific government regulations from agencies such as the FDA, FCC, USDA, etc. If you are doing some level of lobbying, then those are internal things that you are doing to affect the environment. If you are simply monitoring what is happening, then it is a purely external issue.

Internal factors are the proactive actions your company can take to change the market environment. It is possible to use your internal resources to influence environmental factors.

Some examples of internal factors that are at your disposal are:

- Financial resources
- Physical resources
- Human resources
- Intellectual property
- Proprietary processes

The Change Factors Matrix is a very valuable brainstorming tool for you and your team. You can unearth some instructive and valuable results by using this tool in your strategic planning process.

Market Share Projections

Once you have a handle on your target market's size and growth, you will need to forecast your company's revenue and market share. If you are a first mover in your target markets, you will typically start with 100% market share. As the market evolves and competition enters, you will end up with somewhere between 60% and 70% market share over time if you are the market leader, and the product is not a commodity. This is a good assumption for tops-down modeling purposes. If the market is growing fast enough, then you can continue to drive revenue growth even during a period of modest market share loss.

Example of Sizing an Emerging Market Opportunity

When I joined Entropic in 2003, there was no market for multi-room DVR. The DVR market had started to gain good traction in the US with about 30 percent TV household penetration in 2003. My team and I believed and evangelized that every home with more than one TV was a potential market for multi-room DVR – since consumers wanted to be able to fast forward through commercials and record programs for viewing later. The argument was that DVR would eventually penetrate every multi-TV home and consumers would want DVR functionality on every TV in the home. Of course, you could put more than one DVR in the home, which is what Pay TV operators were doing for consumers at the time. However, DVR boxes were about $100 more expensive than a non-DVR set-top box, even if that box did not include MoCA.

During this time, many pay TV operators, including Comcast and Time Warner, would not supply a second DVR to their subscribers. When consumers had multiple DVRs in their home – usually from TiVo – they could not access the movies and TV programs that were stored on the family room DVR at the other rooms in the house, like the master bedroom.

We covered a critical part in this process for investors – stating our assumptions and why we thought those assumptions were valid.

When we did our market forecast, we decided to use multi-TV homes as the TAM and DVR homes as the SAM. Entropic assumed that once a consumer had DVR functionality, they would want it for every TV in the house. Our market would grow, as there were more multi-TV homes and more DVR homes. MoCA-based set-top boxes and MoCA-enabled DVRs were a substitute product for multiple DVRs in the home. We covered a critical part in this process for investors – stating our assumptions and why we thought those assumptions were valid.

There were a lot of skeptics back in those early days. People did not see a need to stream video room-to-room in the home. Over the next couple of years, recognition of the market need did emerge; however, experts felt that another home networking technology like Wi-Fi, or

HomePlug (using the power outlets), or HPNA (using the phone lines) would be dominant.

It wasn't until we deployed with DirecTV in 2010 that people realized that MoCA would be the de facto standard for home networking of streaming video. We won our first deployment with Verizon in 2004 and started deploying in the Verizon FiOS rollout in 2005.

What did we learn from this? Do not let the skeptics get you down if you have done your homework. If you believe in the market opportunity and have a strong value proposition, tune out the naysayers and keep at it.

The Concept of the Product Life Cycle and Its Importance to Forecasting Markets

Although there was no market for multi-room DVR in 2003, there was an established market for DVR, and it had moved from the early adopter market into the mainstream market. By 2010, DVR penetration in the US Pay TV market was close to 80 percent.

In his book *Crossing the Chasm*, author Geoffrey Moore offers a helpful way to think of Product Life Cycle curves as you are entering new

Figure 4.3 - Product Life Cycle

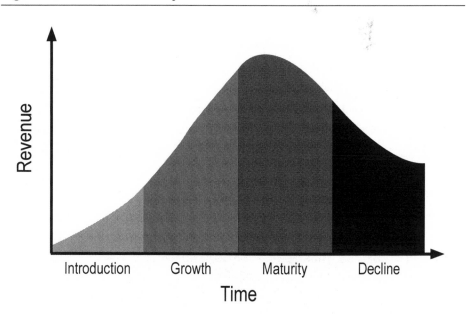

markets. You can see in the figure below that you have the introduction of the product, the growth stage, maturity, and decline.

Moore breaks the customer base down into early adopters in the introduction phase and the early majority in the growth phase. Customers in these two phases of the product life cycle have very different buying characteristics. As such, a so-called chasm exists between the early growth and the explosive growth in a new business. You must have a clear understanding of that and be able to describe why your company is on the cusp of getting into explosive growth. The more that you can clearly show that – not only in financial, quantitative terms, but also in qualitative terms – the more interest you are going to garner from potential investors.

Product life cycle curves are important tools for two pieces of analysis. The first is the **life cycle of a whole market**, for example the time it took for color television sets to go from first adopters of the product to the point where there was market saturation. This market was nearly saturated with 90 percent household penetration in the US by 1986. People who live in the US watch a lot of TV, or at least we used to before the internet, social media and mobile devices!

The second important way to look at product life cycles is for **a given product generation**. In the heyday of the personal computer industry, a new graphics chip was introduced into the market every six months. The time that you could sell a single generation of graphics chips was between 12 and 18 months. That is not a very long time to recoup your investment, even with the very high volume in the PC industry at the time. During this period, there was a consolidation of graphics chips suppliers from over 30 companies down to two. In many cases, the leader in one generation of products would be pushed out of the market within a couple product cycles. It is critically important that you understand the product life cycles in your target market.

The Importance of Market Research

Market research is an essential part of strategic planning. However, the mere idea of conducting market research can overwhelm many entrepreneurs. They think of spending thousands of dollars and countless hours on surveys, focus groups and reports. This is why many startups overlook or even avoid market research. However, market analysis is essential to understanding business opportunity, developing your business strategy, and describing your business model. Market research does not have to be that complicated or expensive, or too time-consuming, as explained below.

Let's look at the two main types of market research.

Primary Market Research: Research you do yourself or as a company.

Secondary Market Research: Research conducted by another company, usually a research firm. The research agency has been called a third party since they sit outside the industry of your company, its customers, your competitors, and other parties that directly interact with your market.

All startups need to do is talk to customers or potential customers. Unfortunately, just talking to customers is not going to result in a business model for an emerging market, since customers are so focused on solving the problems that they have today. Startups must therefore find a way to step back and see things from a broader perspective. As we discussed in the Entropic MoCA example above, you may need to look at related or adjacent markets, like the DVR market, in order to develop a forecast for your market opportunity.

Primary Research

There are two main types of primary market research. First, you can conduct **surveys** of your target customers and other important stakeholders in your ecosystem. Surveys can be in person, written, or online, and can be formal or informal. If done correctly, surveys can provide not only qualitative but also quantitative information. The sample size for a survey needs to be relatively large in order for it to be "statistically significant" on a quantitative basis. The internet has a number of resources, including one from *Creative Survey Systems* which has a "Sample Size Calculator" to determine sample size and confidence factor. However, even surveys where you ask five or ten customers half a dozen questions can be extremely valuable on a qualitative basis. These types of "bellwether" surveys can be very instructive for gathering responses around several qualitative factors that deal with your product, especially if you are polling thought leaders in your vertical markets. A good and inexpensive tool for conducting online surveys is *Survey Monkey*, and *Harvard University* has some good tips on "Survey Questionnaire Design."

The second type of primary research is to conduct target customer **focus groups**, which is a lot more qualitative in nature. They can be very valuable in helping refine your product, especially if you get a good cross of the demographic you are pursuing in your target customer base. Lehigh University has some great tips about "Conducting Focus Groups."

Secondary Research

Contrary to what many entrepreneurs think, secondary research does not have to be expensive. It can be available via various government agencies, trade groups and organizations, business magazines, academic institutions – even a variety of international sources. Many times the research is available for free or at a very low cost, and can be easily accessed online. A great source of data is the US Census, and Wikipedia has a very good list of "Free Online Resources."

Of course, there are bigger and more expensive firms as well – groups like Gartner Group, Forrester, IDC, In-Stat, and a variety of other third-party research organizations that my own businesses have used. Because of the bigger price tags involved with these firms, you need to find creative ways to get the most salient parts of the research without spending a lot of money. Frequently these big research agencies will release some of the key quantitative nuggets from their research in the public domain online, in press releases, and in news articles. The internet makes it easy to find good research if you know how to conduct intelligent searches. One of the biggest tricks with online search is to use the right keywords, long keywords, and phrases. The City University of New York has some good "Methods for Effective Internet Research." Large investment banks are another great source of research, and startups or their advisers can frequently get access to this data simply by asking.

Understanding Your Customers

The next action to take – one that is near and dear to my heart, and one of the top two most important things associated with a situation analysis – is to conduct an assessment of what makes your customers tick. Customer analysis is different from market analysis, because you focus more on the value proposition than size and growth, but they do go hand-in-hand.

This is where you really want to get into your customer's head. You may have heard people talking about developing a customer avatar. According to *HubSpot*, a **customer avatar** is a fictional character that represents your ideal prospect. Once complete, it will help you understand the motivating beliefs, fears and secret desires that influence your **customer's** buying decisions. HubSpot provides a good high-level customer "Avatar Workbook."

Another good tool, available from *Digital Marketer*, is the "Customer Avatar Worksheet." This process helps you to develop a set of demographics related to your customers, and understand their problems from their perspective. When you are doing customer analysis, you want to ask the following questions:

- What is the problem that you are trying to solve for your focus customer?
- What is the relative market share of each of your target customers in your target market?
- Are you dealing with a small number of target customers that have very large market share – or, is it a highly fragmented customer group that does not have much power?
- Are there one or two customers that set the trends in the industry?
- Are some customers more innovative than others?
- What is the revenue trend by customer for three years?
- In a B2B selling situation, are there one or two big players that you need to win in order to be successful in your business?

For instance, if you are selling into the cellular phone industry, it's very important that you win Verizon and AT&T in the US market. The other guys are relatively smaller. If you are selling in Europe, Vodafone is very important.

It's also essential to look at your direct customers and end-customers – these are your customers' customers. Who are the most important ones to win? Can they be a bellwether and a leader for future business?

Your customers' **revenue by region** is another important area of interest. If your solution is specifically targeted for one geographical area, a global competitor might seem extremely strong from a worldwide standpoint, but not very strong in the target geography that you are initially going after. That's important for you to know.

A big part of customer analysis is quantifying the value of your solution. In order to do this, you need to deeply understand the problem you are solving for the customer, from the customers' perspective. How important and large is the problem? How are they currently solving it – if at all? What is the price of the substitute products? What are the value and limitations of existing solutions?

You need to deeply understand the problem you are solving for the customer, from the customers' perspective.

To develop a good understanding of market size and market growth, you need to be a student of your customers' behavior, their needs, their fears, and their concerns – before penetrating a market with your solution. The answers to these questions are based on preliminary feedback from target customers, some market research, your knowledge of the market dynamics based on your domain expertise, your technical knowledge, and an understanding of your customers' problem as it relates to your solution and its alternatives.

The information you gather in customer analysis will allow you to develop preliminary value-based pricing for your product – and you should always work to price your product based on its value to the customer. If customers can reverse engineer the cost of your product, they will sometimes try to get a price that is a standard markup from that cost – this is called cost-plus pricing. When setting pricing for your products or services, you must assess and include the value that you provide into your pricing. Of course, you need to keep in mind that your pricing model is purely hypothetical until you start selling your product and see what customers will pay for it. At this point it is about negotiation. However, if you have done your homework, understand the customers, and have deep domain expertise, your hypothesis should be largely correct.

Customer Analysis Example

While our direct customers at Entropic were set-top manufactures like Motorola and Cisco, we also had to work with their subcontractors. Our end customers were the Pay TV operators. Our customer base was concentrated. Only eight companies controlled the set-top box market, and the top 4 had about 70 percent market share. Additionally, the top five cable operators had 80 percent of the US cable TV business, and there were only two satellite TV providers: DirecTV and Dish Network. Obviously, customers wielded a lot of power – so we had to be solving a fairly big problem to have any chance of getting business.

We had to determine the value of MoCA. If a DVR box cost $100 more than a non-DVR box, would that not mean that a MoCA chip was worth $100? Even if you charged $75 per MoCA chip, would that not still be a big money saver? That math works if you do not consider substitute products and new entrants. At the time, Wi-Fi chips were selling for $7 to $12; even the highest end Wi-Fi was $15. Ethernet, another data networking technology, cost less than $1 per box, but it required rewiring of the house. Broadcom told customers that if they waited for their integrated MoCA on their set-top processor chip, it would be under $10. We ended up with pricing in the mid-teens with a price curve that moved to under $10 per chip with time and volume. We knew that integration of MoCA functionality was inevitable; since Broadcom was late with MoCA integration on their chip, we were able to "cross the chasm" into mainstream deployments by offering MoCA discrete chips integrated into set-top boxes. As such, we had established MoCA as a de facto industry standard for networking of video in the home.

Understanding the Competitive Landscape

Competitive analysis has two components:

- Competitiveness of the specific **product** in terms of relative price-performance and product features
- Competitiveness on a **company** level, related to depth and breadth of entire product lines, relationships with customers and with suppliers

You need to look critically at where you sit in comparison to your competition.

I always encourage the inclusion of new or potential new entrants to the market as well as potential substitute products in any competitive analysis. This kind of "relative competition" can put a cap on your pricing as shown in the example above.

Competitive Product Features Analysis

A product feature is an attribute of your solution. This is sometimes part of the product specification; however, it can also be pricing, the way the product is used, and the partner ecosystem around the product. For example, features of an automobile can include four doors, bucket seats, sunroof, Bluetooth, heated seats, and the like.

You need to answer the following questions when comparing what you offer to the competition:

- How do you compare on **product features**?
- What is your **product cost structure** relative to the competition?
- Where do you sit today versus where you might sit in the future? What is your **product roadmap and timeline**?
- What do your various **competitors' product roadmaps** look like?

It is not always easy to get all of this information. In order to answer these questions, you will need to do some competitive product surveillance. Talk to customers, suppliers, and other companies in your industry ecosystem. Find out what the most likely product roadmaps are for your potential or direct competitors. Talking to a variety of people within a large customer organization can help you piece together the competitive puzzle. Read trade magazines and any other key publications that your target customers and competitors are reading.

The next step is to do a Competitive Product Features analysis. In this table – shown below – you list your firm's and your competitors' products in the top row, and catalog features important to your customer in the left-hand column. A competitive product feature comparison is one of the best ways to help investors understand how your solution stacks up against alternatives.

It is quite possible that as a startup, you have no direct competition. However, this tool can still be very valuable; just list alternative solutions or substitutes, along with potential new entrants, as possible solutions for

Table 4.2 - Competitive Product Features

	Your Company	Competitor A	Competitor B	Competitor C
Feature 1				
Feature 2				
Feature 3				
Feature 4				
Feature 5				

comparison purposes. All features critical to a customer should be listed in this table. The comparison can be as easy as using yes and no criteria. Depending on whether you have or do not have that feature, you can just put a checkbox in the table, or leave it blank. You can also weight how well you meet a required feature. You might use a scale from 1 to 5, where 1 says you barely meet the requirement and 5 says you have fully met it. If you do a weighting, you should include a legend that explains it.

Another approach to competitive product features analysis is to rank order product features by importance to the customer. This can simply be highest to lowest; however, it's even more instructive to group features together into so-called must-have features that are essential to winning the business versus like-to-have features. Color-coding can help in rank ordering, as long as you include a legend, if you think that it will be valuable to your audience to help understand the information better. The corresponding benefit describes why that feature is valuable to your customer.

Product Features/Benefits Analysis

A Product Features-Benefits analysis is complementary to a Competitive Product Features analysis. A particular feature's benefit tells the customer what problem the product is solving for them – and therefore expresses the value of that feature to the customer.

A product feature/benefit analysis is a useful sales tool, since it translates what your product does into a language that the customer understands and cares about. However, be cautious about how you describe and quantify the value of your product to a customer – you want to describe value without appearing to know the customer's business better than they do. Since a product feature/benefit analysis helps to describe your value proposition,

Table 4.3 - Product Features/Benefits

Feature	Benefit

this tool can also be valuable for discussions about your products with prospective investors. A solid feature/benefit analysis requires an intimate understanding of the problem you are trying to solve, the specifics of how your solution solves the problem, and the ultimate value that you deliver from providing that solution. An example for Entropic's MoCA solution is:

- Feature: Sufficient dynamic range and multi-path mitigation for a signal to work backwards though cable splitters with signal integrity.
- Benefit: MoCA allows you to move video room-to-room in a house.

I cannot tell you the number of times that an entrepreneur does not do this translation of the feature to the corresponding customer benefit, and this creates at least two issues. First, the customer is left to do the translation, and second, you will never know the value of your product unless you clearly understand the problem that you are solving.

To describe a customer benefit, you need to deeply understand the value of the solution to the customer. If a product has appeal in more than one product market segment, the feature/benefit analysis can be different for each. A feature and its associated benefit can translate into value for the customer – which then translates into product unit price, if you are implementing a so-called value-based pricing philosophy. This in turn translates into gross margin.

What do I mean by that? While the cost of the product is the same regardless of whom you are selling it to, you might be able to sell it for a higher price to customers for whom it has higher value – and that translates into higher gross margins and better profitability. I recall a specific situation in the specialty chemical industry. The company had a basic chemical product that had over 1,000 different Stock Keeping Units, or SKUs. The product was sold in everything from 3-ounce quantities to 55-gallon drums. It had different product names and numbers for different applications. It was sold through a dozen different market channels that served different market segments and different customer groups. Depending on the application of the product, it had different warranties. Not all pricing differentiation or discrimination schemes need to be this sophisticated, but there are clearly opportunities for some level of price differentiation for different customers. You do have to guard against so-called arbitrage situations, and ideally make sure there are some added product features to help with the price differentiation. In a simpler case in the semiconductor chip business, we did price differentiation based on volume, terms of sale, additive software features, and feature or time-based exclusivity. The benefit your product offers is a key consideration for pricing – along with competition and other market forces. This is important to investors because it translates into higher gross margins, bigger profits, and increased value of the company.

Let's take a look at some examples of features and benefits. A feature might be, "Greek yogurt is nutritious and packed with protein." The corresponding benefit is, "Choosing Greek yogurt makes you healthier and more satisfied."

A feature could be, "This medicine has 500 mg of acetaminophen." The corresponding benefit, "One dose of this medicine will relieve your headache and allow you to enjoy your day."

A feature could be, "This phone case is made with layers of carbon fiber and reinforced plastic." The benefit: "If you drop your phone in this case, it will survive a fall from any reasonable distance."

Competitors on a Company-to-Company Basis

Of course, you need to look beyond product feature comparisons at a broader set of issues when assessing the competition. You need to do a full Competitor Analysis.

Table 4.4 - Competitive Analysis

	Your Company	Competitor A	Competitor B	Competitor C
Strategy				
Product Line				
Size				
Channels				
Capabilities				

This includes your overall strategy versus your competitors'; the relative breadth of your product lines; relative company size; market channel strategy, in other words your presence or geographic focus versus competition; manufacturing strategy; and other capabilities. Some key questions to ask and answer include:

- What is your cost position versus competitors?
- Are you going to be the low cost leader or are you competing more at a product differentiation level?

- What is the importance of your solution and your company to your customer?
- Are you providing a solution that they really need – or are they going to discard you at the first opportunity?

Providing an offering that customers want and will pay for is not only about winning the first design and getting that initial revenue momentum. It's about sustaining value and importance for your company over the longer term, which allows you to last more than one product generation.

Our largest potential direct competitor at Entropic was Broadcom – even before they started working on MoCA. If you were competing in communications semiconductors and you were not competing with Broadcom, you were probably in a small and uninteresting market. They would go after anything that looked as if it were a reasonable enough size.

Entropic was a "focus" competitor, while Broadcom was a "broad-based" competitor. Broadcom had significant power with many of the customers that Entropic was pursuing. So we not only had to compete on a product features-benefits basis, we also had to overcome the Broadcom incumbency position in adjacent technologies and their promise to deliver an alternative solution to Entropic, even though they did not yet have a suitable solution for the customer. This so-called "engage and delay" strategy is commonly used by an incumbent competitor to keep new suppliers and startups from gaining any traction with the customer base. The best answer for this strategy is stellar execution on your product plan. You need to consider this when you are looking at the overall competitive situation; it's not just a battle on the product level, but at the overall company level as well.

Industry Structure Analysis

As mentioned in the previous chapter, industry structure analysis – also known as Porter's Five Forces Analysis – is useful for assessing the current situation as part of a strategic planning process. The five forces in Industry Structure Analysis are:

- Buyer power
- Supplier power

- Threat of substitutes
- Threat of new entrants
- Competitive rivalry

In Industry Structure Analysis you look at your company's power relative to the five forces. Although it is a simple tool, it is very effective for identifying and understanding where the power lies in your industry. Power is largely a relative number game. For example, if there aren't that many competitors, that is a good thing. Having a large number of customers relative to the number of competitors is a positive thing in an industry. It is good if you have a large number of customers or large number of suppliers relative to those competitors. The other major component is about barriers to entry and exit for the market. Those factors can also determine the relative attractiveness of a market. That said, very few startups and entrepreneurs are applying this tool to their business to gain critical insight and understanding. The insight gained from doing Industry Structure Analysis can not only improve your chances of business success, but will also increase your chances of getting funded, primarily due to your improved understanding of your business model today and how it is likely to evolve over time. It can even lead to key insights such as not having a viable business model, in which case you should either pivot or abandon the business. It is better to fail fast and not lose much money versus spending a ton of money and having nothing to show for it except many upset investors.

Michael Porter developed the Industry Structure Analysis tool based on the observation that profit margins vary between industries, which can be explained by the structure of an industry. Although the concept of industry structure analysis has been around for a long time, Michael Porter popularized a model in his book *Competitive Strategy* that is especially relevant to strategic planning. Porter also outlines the ways that companies compete. It is a foundational book in the area of strategy, and I highly encourage all entrepreneurs to read it.

One thing to keep in mind is that based on empirical evidence, the standard deviation of profits **within** an industry is even **greater** than the profit distribution **across** industries. In other words, if you are the dominant player in a given target market, you will typically command higher profits than the other competitors in your market space. This observation is what prompted former General Electric CEO Jack Welch to state, "GE will be #1 or #2 within any business where it competes." If you are not in the top two competitors, you do not make very much money.

Industry structure analysis can help you understand how to position and price your product or service, and where the power base exists in your target market. You want to have an attractive industry structure AND be the dominant player in your niche to achieve the highest profits for your company.

MindTools gives a good summary of "Porter's Five Forces," but I recommend reading Porter's books *Competitive Strategy* and *Competitive Advantage* for any CEO or business owner.

Industry Structure Analysis is extremely instructive for any business – even startups. Merely undertaking the thought process associated with a Porter Five Forces Analysis provides value – whether you are a small business going after a retail opportunity or a technology business trying to displace incumbent solutions with something that performs better or has a more attractive cost. It does not take days to conduct this analysis; you can do it over an afternoon, and get a good feel for things.

SWOT Analysis

A SWOT Analysis consists of strengths, weaknesses, opportunities, and threats, conducted via two sets of analyses. The first requires that you assess strengths and weaknesses of your competitive position, your product leadership, your customer relationships, and your geographic positioning.

The next part is to consider opportunities and threats. What scenarios are available for competitive tactics and strategy? How are your competitors going to react to you entering or changing the market? What is the threat of new entrants or substitutes? Can you capitalize on your competitors' weaknesses and the industry structure? You will notice that much of the opportunities and threats analysis will naturally flow from your PESTEL and industry structural analysis.

The Situation of Your Team and Organization

Assessing your company's current situation also requires you to look at things in the **marketing and sales function** – such as:

- Sales coverage
- Health of your customer relationships
- Your sales team's technical competence
- Your marketing team's market knowledge

Use any competitive benchmarks available to make an assessment and ask what you can do to get better, specifically concerning the following functions:

Look at your **operations team**. How do you deal with your suppliers? How do you stack up against competition in areas like delivery, product costs, quality, reliability, and competitive benchmarks?

Next, you should have strong **finance, legal, and human resources** functions. In many cases, especially with early stage companies, you can outsource this to capable professionals. However, you should develop an in-house capability in these areas as you grow your company in order to have the right level of controls, accountability, and a unified culture.

Look at your **product development team** and **core technology** situation. Are you building products designed for testability and re-use – allowing you to leverage your R&D dollars further? Are they designed for manufacturability and scalability? In other words, can you fan out to a much broader set of customers rapidly because you have scalability in your product or manufacturability in the case of a hardware-oriented product? Again, are competitive benchmarks available?

Finally, look at the people you have got on board, and ask, "Who are the key players on this team, and what are their track records?" Investors are usually going to ask this. If you have a relatively young and inexperienced team, do you have mentors and advisers whose experience you can leverage to "trade-up" for track record? You want to be able to claim, "Our team has the brightest technical experts in the world. Although we're less experienced, we have some extremely successful, solid people with very strong track records around us – and we're working closely with them."

Are some of these people on your **board of directors**? What are their accomplishments? Is the team itself a competitive advantage, neutral – or is it a weakness? If it is a neutral or a negative, you need to work on this immediately.

You are going to have detailed information about your markets, customers, and competitors after you complete a situation analysis. You will have an explanation of where you fit within the overall ecosystem of your industry, a description of how your solution solves a critical customer problem, your unique value proposition, knowledge of how your product stacks up against competition, and how your company stacks up against competitors. The next step in the strategic planning process is to understand your financial goals, likely financial restrictions, and have a first pass at your financial plans. Money is the fuel that will allow your company to grow. If you cannot fuel this growth out of revenue alone, then you will need to raise outside capital. Knowing how much money and why you need it is critically important to prospective investors.

CHAPTER 5

Available Provisions for the Journey

The next element of your strategic plan is determining your financial goals. As we all know, there is not an unlimited amount of capital available to fund your startup, so you will need to show a business model that will deliver acceptable results with a reasonable amount of invested capital. You will also need to make assumptions about how much capital you will have available to your company. You have completed your situation analysis, where we have looked in detail at your market, your customers, the competitive landscape, and have a topographical map of the market landscape and where your company fits on that map. Now you need to look at your financial goals and scope available and desired financial resource, which indirectly includes your headcount plan. This is the way that investors will ultimately measure your results in business terms once your financial goals become a financial plan.

Figure 5.1 - Strategic Planning Process - Financial Goals

The stages of progress for a startup company include:

- Ideation
- Development, Pre-Product and Pre-Revenue
- Initial Prototypes, Pre-Revenue
- Product Samples, Beta Testing, and Pre-Revenue
- Initial Revenue from One or a Small Number of Early Access Customers
- Customer Diversification and Expansion with Your First Product
- Product Roadmap Execution and Continued Diversification
- Product Diversification and Expansion

The stages of investment in a startup are:

- Bootstrapping (i.e., using your own funds)
- Getting funds from Friends & Family
- Seed Investment – Usually Angel Investment
- Series A – Angel Round or first VC Round
- Series B (growth) – VC lead or Alternative Financing
- Series C (growth/expansion) – VC lead or Alternative Financing

Ideally, you will not need additional financing rounds after a Series C, but sometimes there are additional rounds, or an IPO. There are also equity crowdfunding alternatives for companies based on the *U.S. JOBS Act*. This is discussed in detail at the end of this chapter.

You should apply "lean startup" principles to any somewhat new venture. This is about more than being frugal; it is about testing ideas with real customers at various stages of new product development to gain customer feedback, insight, and direction.

In the book *The Lean Startup*, author Eric Reis talks about a concept he calls the Minimum Viable Product. This product goes beyond the prototype phase, and is one that you can sell to some subset of your target market. According to Reis, it is also the product where you can do the "maximum amount of validated learning with the highest return on investment versus risk." This means you have a customer with a relatively low customer acquisition cost who can and does give you opinions about how to improve your product that has broad market importance. Getting customer comments early and frequently can save you a lot of time and money, and it just makes good business sense. In this way you can test, validate, and refine your unique value proposition and even commercialize the product to drive initial revenue. Many of the ideas in *The Lean Startup* have been around for decades, but Reis has a way of packaging them that makes them easy to understand and digest for today's entrepreneurs.

Once you are beyond the bootstrapping and friends & family stage, you should raise money in 18 to 24 month increments. You want enough cash "runway" to accomplish some key milestones, and investors will want to see some substantial and measurable progress over a 12 to 18 month period. Since you should count on needing at least six months to raise an institutional funding round, you want to have six months of cash "runway" while you are working to raise your subsequent funding round. You will only get a step up in valuation if you have made material progress against key milestones, shown additional proof of your business model, and reduced risk. This makes the set of milestones in the first 12 months after a financing critical.

Most startup companies should have a **three-year** strategic plan. This allows you to show a product roadmap and revenue ramp during the planning cycle. Some investors may want to see a five-year plan, and some technologies and life science sector products may take longer than three years to generate revenue if you are raising money in a relatively early stage in the life of the company. As discussed earlier in the book, you can extrapolate years four and five from year three if you need to show a five-year plan.

You want to set and accomplish **financial goals** with a given amount of capital over a given amount of time. **Financial constraints** are the available amount of capital over a given amount of time. You set a **financial plan** once you undergo an iterative process that helps you determine how much you can accomplish with that money – considering other factors like product development time, product adoption time by customers, and hiring key talent. You will have a high-level financial plan at the end of the strategic planning process that will get more specific for the first 12 months when you do your Annual Operating Plan, or AOP, and budget.

As the leader of your startup, you should expect a return on your investment for your sweat equity, as well as the money you put into the business. Outside investors are also expecting a return on investment. They want to see how your business model works, in financial terms; how much capital you need to meet your goals; and how you are planning to use the money you are requesting from them. Angel investors and venture capitalists do not expect an instant return, but they do expect progress toward the goals over any reasonable time.

Some key questions to consider are:

- What are the **explicit and implicit components** of your financial goals and plan?
- What are the **key financial metrics** critical for running a startup business?
- What **additional financial metrics** are important to prospective investors?
- What is a **realistic amount of capital** available to your company?

Key financial goals include information like revenue projections, gross margin projections, projected operating expenses and operating margins, capital requirements, working capital requirements, and cash flow resulting from the business. You should be able to produce a pro-forma income statement and balance sheet; however, the most important pieces of strategic planning are the P&L, capital budget, and cash flow plan.

Your financial goals need to go hand-in-hand with your key milestones. In other words, if you are hiring a product development team to work on your project, you will have headcount and non-headcount related expenses associated with the project. You should expect to complete the project in a certain timeframe, and incur expenses at a certain stage of the product's development. Once the product is commercialized, you should expect to incur marketing and sales expenses and generate revenue in a certain timeframe that depends upon your specific sales cycle. When you are looking forward to raising outside capital, it is important to include your funding request and use of funds.

It's always a good idea to test your business model by doing "scenario analysis" and "sensitivity analysis." Typical revenue scenarios are a base case, an upside case, and a downside case. It is best to set the base case of revenue at the 90 percent confidence level in the current year, especially if there is no track record of historical revenue. Expectation management is one of the most important things you need to do as an entrepreneur. It is always better to under commit and over deliver. How you look at an upside and downside forecast depends a lot upon the specifics of your business, but a good rule of thumb is to set the upside forecast based on reasonable upside opportunities. Likewise, the downside case should be based on a reasonable set of things that could go wrong. Do not set upsides and downsides based on everything going right and everything going wrong, respectively – it will make you look out of control of your business. I realize that many things in the startup world are outside our control, but you have to take responsibility and leadership as the leader of your startup. Stating your assumptions about what goes into the baseline, upside and downside is critical. For the purposes of revenue scenarios, a lot depends on your particular business, and this requires domain expertise as well as general business knowledge. Key things to consider are the **conversion rate** of the opportunities in your sales funnel and **churn rate** of existing customers. Conversion rate is the percentage of customer opportunities that you convert to revenue in a given period. Churn is the percentage of customers that discontinue doing business with you over a given period. The more success you have, the more data you will get on conversion rate and churn. These numbers do not have to be fixed. You can implement processes to increase conversion rate and reduce churn. As you do this, you will have the opportunity to refine and optimize your business model.

It may be worthwhile to see how the financial picture changes if your product development takes 25 percent longer than your original projects. Another significant area to test sensitivity is with pricing and cost of goods sold, which ultimately results in changes in gross margins.

Gross Margin = (ASP-COGS)/ASP

How much of an impact will a 10 percent increase or decrease in Average Selling Price (ASP) or Cost of Goods Sold (COGS) have on your overall financial projections? If investors get interested in your business, they will run some of this analysis on your financial projections – so you need to have a clear idea of how this works and be able to intelligently answer questions they ask about it.

Revenue Basics with the Investor in Mind

The most important part of any growth company's financial summary is revenue projections. Keep in mind that calculation of revenue is simple:

Revenue = (Product Unit Volume) X ASP

Investors will critically scrutinize your revenue forecast more than any other thing, so you need to devote enough attention to revenue to answer difficult questions and defend your assumptions – without becoming defensive, of course!

The higher the ASP of your product, the fewer units you need to sell in order to generate the same revenue. While you may not have a business that garners extremely high ASPs, the unit volume available in your market could be massive – or it could be that the unit volume is somewhat smaller, but ASPs are quite high. An example of a low price product is a piece of software that sells as Software as a Service (SaaS) for a monthly subscription of $10. An example of an extremely low price product is a resistor that is assembled onto an electronics printed circuit board, and may have a price of just a few cents. An example of an extremely high price product is a Boeing 777, which has a list price of $261.5 million, and this is the lowest price model of the 777 aircraft! These all can be good business models, as long as the revenue growth has the potential to be explosive, gross margins are healthy, and there is operating leverage in your business model. We will discuss more about this in a minute, but let's look at explosive growth revenue forecast credibility first.

The "Hockey Stick" Revenue Forecast

I have looked at hundreds of startup financial projections over my career – and pretty much every one I have ever seen has this so-called "hockey stick" revenue growth. This makes sense if you are addressing a market with potentially explosive growth. However, there needs to be some rationale as to the timing of the aggressive ramp.

When I listen to these investor presentations, I am waiting for the rationale of why the revenue curve accelerates at a particular point, and I am typically disappointed that there is not any real reason. Most presenters have no explanation for why the revenue automatically hockey sticks at that particular time. They might as well put on the slide: "The Miracle Happens Here."

Figure 5.2 - "Hockey Stick" Revenue Growth

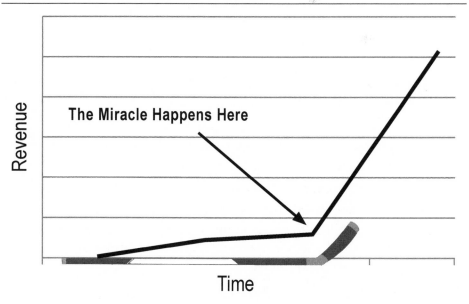

As a startup CEO, you do not want to do this! It will be one of the biggest mistakes that you can make and it will undermine your credibility with prospective investors. However, you must forecast rapid revenue growth at some point to garner interest from Angel investors and venture capitalists. Obviously, this presents a dilemma, and therein lies the conundrum. The answer is that you must have qualitative support for why the revenue accelerates at that particular point. A concept that is helpful to understand is reaching a "tipping point." The tipping point is a marketing concept developed by Malcolm Gladwell in his book *The Tipping Point*. This concept plays off the idea that a small action, such as nudging a domino, causes a large chain reaction. It is similar to when things go "viral" on the internet. Interestingly, there is no agreed-upon definition of what constitutes going viral. YouTube personality Kevin "Nalts" Nalty said in 2011, "A few years ago, a video could be considered 'viral' if it hit a million views, but now only if it gets more than 5 million views in a 3–7 day period" can it be considered viral. So be careful how you characterize your explosive growth and what language you use. The bigger key here is that adoption takes on a life of its own, but it is important to explain why. What is important about these concepts from a revenue acceleration standpoint is that your solution is understood and valued on a widespread basis. A good indication that you have reached this status is that people, or more importantly, a significant percentage of customers in your target market, have "heard" about your solution and already have a basic understanding of what it does when someone else mentions it.

Startup success is like growing bamboo. Initially it looks as if it is not growing at all, but after a couple of years it shoots up and grows faster than any other tree. As a friend of mine likes to say, "You do not give birth to adults." New startups are like little babies; they need to be fed and nurtured before they can grow to produce results. Yet another key concept to understand is moving from the early adopter stage to the early majority stage in the product life cycle, as Geoffrey Moore describes in his book Crossing the Chasm, which we discussed in Chapter 4 as it related to product life cycles.

Some explanations for the acceleration of revenue can be:

- **Landing the Industry Leader**: In a B2B business, gaining adoption by a large customer that is ramping your product rapidly can drive significant growth, and just as importantly, the adoption by the industry leader may lead other key customers to adopt your solution as well.
- **Proof of Concept at Scale**: An early adopter customer goes into production with your product or service and it validates the value proposition of your solution. You use that data in case studies and testimonials, and incorporate that into your promotional materials. You get rapid acceptance of your solution by additional customers that provide even more validation.
- **Expert or Thought Leader Endorsement**: Similar to adoption by an early adopter customer, the public endorsement by an industry expert or thought leader provides validation of your solution to their audience. If the expert's audience overlaps with your target customer base, this validation can pave the way for accelerated revenue.
- **Reaching a Critical Cost or Price Point**: In this case, customers are using your solution in a limited way, then it reaches a sufficient volume or achieves learning economies to "break through" to a lower cost, which enables a lower price and opens up a set of much higher-volume applications.
- **Government Body Approval**: In this case, government approval is required for either widespread use or even for your solution to be used at all. Examples here are a drug that gets FDA approval, or a communications technology that gets FCC approval.
- **Finding a New High Volume Usage Model**: In 1989, at the drug company Pfizer, scientists Peter Dunn and Albert Wood created a drug called sildenafil citrate that they believed would be useful in treating high blood pressure and angina, a chest pain associated with coronary heart disease. This drug later became Viagra, which is used to treat erectile dysfunction, apparently a very high volume market opportunity.

In any situation where you show acceleration in your revenue forecast, for it to be taken seriously by investors you need to clearly state your assumptions. Keep in mind that it is not uncommon to grow in "spurts." You may get a burst in revenue then plateau before getting your next burst. There can also be "lumpiness" in revenue growth. This can frequently be attributed to seasonality in your end market. Regardless of what you show in your revenue forecast, you need to be able to state your assumptions and be prepared to explain and defend them.

Fundamentals for Building a Credible Revenue Forecast

A credible long-term revenue forecast needs to be based on a combination of **tops-down** support, based on your **market size; growth and market share** assumptions that you detailed in your situation analysis; and a **bottoms-up** analysis based on your **sales funnel**.

A **solid tops-down forecast** does not just look at the market size and assign a percentage. Even in tops-down analysis, you need to look at potential customers from an opportunity standpoint, even if they have not entered your sales funnel. After all, target customers are what make up your markets. In a solid tops-down forecast, you need to answer the following:

- **How big can each customer be**? Customers, even if they are individuals, can come in varying sizes. You may offer a tiered set of products or services. In B2B businesses, like the tech companies that I used to run, some customers buy a lot more units than others.
- What is the **average deal or transaction size**?
- **How many customers** will you need to win to achieve a certain level of sales?
- Do you have the **sales and support** reaches to convert that many customers?
- Do you have the **market channels** to win and support that number of customers?
- What is your **conversion rate**, also known as success rate, "hit rate" or "flow through rate"? In other words – how many customers do you need to contact to convert a customer?
- What is the **churn rate**, as a percentage, for those customers?

This thought process helps you validate your market size, and provides substantial credibility to your story. Don't be the entrepreneur who says, "All I have to do is get 3 percent of this $1 billion market, and

I am golden." In a **credible bottoms-up forecast,** you are looking at the **customers in your sales funnel** – specifically, what is going on with them at each phase.

Key questions you should answer include:

Figure 5.3 - Sales Funnel

- How many customers are you reaching in the **awareness** phase?
- How many of those are showing **interest** by asking more questions and seeking out information?
- How many of those are asking for product samples or **evaluating the product?**
- How many of those are resulting in **sales?**
- What is the potential revenue per customer in the **initial transaction?**
- What is a **customer's lifetime value (LTV)?**

Traditional ways to create awareness include advertising, press releases, and writing op-ed articles for newspapers and magazines that target your audience. However, content marketing and online advertising are becoming increasingly important. You must have ways to convert awareness into interest. A lot of businesses give something away for free to get the customers on their mailing list, or email list. Email marketing strategies are becoming more important and sophisticated. However, to not be considered SPAM, you need to make sure you are adding value with everything that you send to current and prospective customers. Social media and email marketing are opportunities to connect with parts of your audience that you may never get to meet in person, and help them get to know, like and trust you. In my blog, I give tons of insights away for free; the same is true of my free webinars. Bottom-line, although you do not want to be too promotional, you need to be willing to promote things that are important to you, and you do not need to apologize for being promotional in those cases, even if some people complain. After all, this is your business. You may get some complaints, and you may get some people who unsubscribe to your list. It happens. Look for trends, and solicit feedback from people you trust. If you get a few people unsubscribing from your email list, it is not a big issue. The focus should be on growing your list in aggregate and conversions.

Once you have engaged with a customer through a product evaluation or a free, feature-reduced version of your product, you need to close them. There are literally hundreds of books about sales, and some real gurus out there in the industry on the topic. Some of my favorites include Tom Hopkins, Zig Ziglar, and Brian Tracy. However, the two best sales books I have ever read are *How to Win Friends and Influence People* by Dale Carnegie, and *Conceptual Selling* by Robert Miller and Stephen Heiman.

Reasonable revenue projections should also account for your solution's **product development cycle**, plus the **sales cycle**, two factors that deal with revenue timing. The product development cycle is the time that it takes from your product development kickoff to the actual production state. The sales cycle is the timeframe from engaging with a customer for initial samples, initial trials or demonstrations to the point where they are buying the product in volume production. I like to say, "It takes nine months to have a baby once you are pregnant. You can't rush it. That's how long it takes!"

However, there are a few scenarios that can speed things up. For example, in a B2B environment, if customers are clamoring for your product and you can have them start to design their solutions around yours, you may be able to run a part of the product development cycle and the sales cycle in parallel.

Maybe you are at an alpha or a beta stage of your product – not quite in a production stage. Because the customer is so excited about using your product, they might start developing and designing it into their products more quickly. Of course this typically takes place in a B2B situation. This was the case of our customer Motorola with Entropic's MoCA solution, since Motorola's customer Verizon was working against a hard deadline to launch their FiOS TV service.

In other cases, the product development cycle and sales cycle need to run in series. In other words, the sales cycle begins when the product is fully commercialized. When you look at time to revenue in this scenario, you have to account for the full period from the start of development to when the product goes into production with the customer.

A true bottoms-up revenue forecast requires a credible sales funnel and a good understanding of the **sales cycle**. You must be constantly interacting with your target customers. Another component is how quickly new customers can **ramp** into volume and what **run-rate revenue** each can sustain. Again, basing this analysis on customer feedback, and analysis of how those target customers traditionally ramp to production, makes it more credible. Statement of your assumptions is a key part of this analysis. Bottoms-up analysis is essential for any credibility in short-term forecasts. Many product companies require **backlog** – orders that customers have already placed with your company – to have any standing in short-term product revenue forecasts.

It can sound like an arduous process – I know. However, once you have won a customer the first time – and they know, like and trust you – making additional sales to them will be a lot easier. They have already gone through the awareness part of the sales funnel. You cannot take this for granted, though – especially if a customer knows you for one thing, and not for another. Keeping customers aware of what you do and what you offer is very important. If you are selling something that is not a repeat of the first transaction, then you need to educate the customer about the new offering. If they can naturally see how a successful experience in the first product leads to your capability in the new offering, then you are ahead of the game. Of course, if the customer has a bad experience, then the reverse is true – and often amplified. A bad customer experience not only leads to no repeat sales; it also frequently leads the dissatisfied customer to give poor reviews of you and your product. This amplifier can be even bigger with the internet, social media, and review websites.

The next step of reasonable revenue growth projections is customer diversification. Once you have that initial customer ramping into production, getting additional customers ramping as well accelerates the revenue growth. One of the best strategies for gaining additional customers is promoting the validation of your value proposition with your existing customers. This can be done through customer testimonials, case studies, and white papers. Of course, it is critical that you do not violate the confidentiality of your existing customers in these promotional efforts.

Finally, projection of quarterly revenue is very instructive when building forecast versus purely annual forecast. Startups usually provide quarterly forecasts for the first year and annual forecasts for the subsequent years. I will typically take the fourth quarter of revenue for the first year, multiply it by four, and see how that looks relative to the second year of revenue projections. If there is no growth – or ridiculously excessive growth – I try to understand what underlies this. If you have already done that work and have supported your annual revenue forecast with quarterly models, the forecasts are more likely to make sense. As such, you will be able to explain them in greater detail when prospective investors or your board starts asking questions about them.

Projection of Gross Margins

The next financial goal is **target gross margins**. As mentioned earlier, as you work your way down the income statement or the profit & loss statement, or P&L, gross margin represents the ASP minus COGS divided by the ASP. Recall that corporate gross margins are a result of all your product revenue minus cost of goods sold.

Gross margin indicates the value of your product to your customers. Interestingly, a product that has a high ASP, but a low gross margin, is not very valuable. Many new entrepreneurs fail to grasp this concept. Revenue growth without gross margin is nice for vanity points, but it is not a real business. You cannot make money in a business unless you have healthy gross margins. Therefore, understanding what drives your average selling price, cost of goods sold, and gross margin, is essential for being able to credibly discuss any financial goals or plan.

In some markets, your initial engagement with your first customers might result in a fairly low gross margin. This is usually due to high COGS, since you have not achieved economies of scale or maybe learning economies, which will result in gross margin expansion. Learning Effect leads to fall in the cost of production per unit because with the increased involvement in the production process your company becomes increasingly familiar with the production process. This leads to improvement in your efficiency level. This is different from economies of scale that are purely a result of driving more volume and the resulting reduction in unit cost.

Gross margin expansion, or systematically increasing your gross margins, is crucial under these circumstances. Even if they are unacceptably low when you first start selling products, you can garner interest from investors if you can show a business model where they expand over time. I have worked with a number of companies where it was very clear that we would benefit from scale economies and learning economies as we scaled the business – and we *did* achieve gross margin expansion.

Finally, your dollar gross margin is more important than percentage gross margin; after all, you want to make money. However, some investors will be fixated on percentage gross margins, so you need to make sure that they are healthy. Investors will compare your gross margins to other similar companies in your market space, even if they are not direct competitors. It is their way of gauging your business model – so you should do competitive benchmarking.

Operating Expenses & Capital Requirements

Next on the income statement is operating expenses. Costs tend to be low when you first launch your startup; after all, how much does it cost for two guys who do not get paid to work in their garage? Maybe you need a few pads of paper and a box of pens at first. However, business expenses grow over time. Eventually, you move beyond the concept and early product prototyping phase – and this requires additional capital and people.

There are a few big buckets of expenses that you should understand at a high level as the CEO of a company:

- Research and Development (R&D) expenses, sometimes called product development cost

- Marketing and Sales (M&S) expenses
- General and Administrative (G&A) expenses

However, time is the most precious commodity in the startup world. You cannot create more time, and it always marches forward. Your customers will not wait for you, and your competitors will try to catch you. You have to make choices every day about where to focus and what to leave behind. There are significant opportunity and inefficiency costs. You must be as productive as is humanly possible.

Of course, there are the direct costs of a startup as well; but you also need to consider hidden costs even in these large buckets. The most significant cost buckets are listed below. I see so many startups being "penny wise and pound foolish." A big part of this is how investors and boards of directors frequently focus on the minutiae rather than the big picture. Try to keep an eye on both the details and high-level strategy as you work out the following seven significant expenses that nearly all startup companies have to consider. Be lean, but be smart.

(1) People

Headcount cost is one of, if not the, highest expense area for most companies. If your company does not own its own manufacturing, it is likely that headcount will be the highest expense item for your startup. Although the finance types like to just call it headcount to dehumanize it, we are talking about real people. Making a decision to bring a person into your company as a full-time employee should be one of the most thoughtful decisions you will make as a startup CEO or founder. Although finance people consider headcount as a variable cost, as a manager and leader you should think about it as a fixed cost – in other words, you plan to keep this employee forever. One of the most difficult and painful things that you can do as a manager is have to lay off employees. Only hire the people that you need over the long term, and contract the rest. Only hire for critical skill sets and to build your core competencies.

Headcount is so important for resource planning, it is essential that you do a separate exercise around headcount planning and your hiring plan, and stick with it. Do not use excess budget in other areas to justify additional hiring. Make each hiring decision based on your company needs, and make sure each hire has the right skill set and fits with the culture you are trying to build in your company. We will discuss this more in Chapter 9 about Building a Winning Team.

Remember, people costs include more than just salaries, payroll taxes and benefits. You also need to pay for scouting, recruiting, hiring, and onboarding – all areas that are frequently forgotten or overlooked when figuring out initial expenses.

Headcount is so important for resource planning, it is essential that you do a separate exercise around headcount planning and your hiring plan.

The war for talent is one of the most significant investment areas for any startup, and you start to incur these costs as soon as you make the decision to hire people. All of these things have direct cost and opportunity costs, on top of what you pay for your own and your co-founders' salaries, and eventually, other employees. The right way to look at people cost is on a fully loaded cost basis that accounts for benefits, facilities, insurance, IT, and the like.

The importance of making people as productive as possible as quickly as possible is paramount. You should also have a goal or plan for the kind of corporate culture you want to develop and encourage, and make sure this is part of the screening and hiring process. Startups are much like a team sport; you need to have productive individuals and productive teams to win.

(2) Facilities & Administration

At some point, you need to move out of the garage and into an office. A workplace includes expenses like tenant improvements (TIs) that you may need to complete to make facilities suitable for your purpose. You will have rent, utilities, communications, IT, furniture, and supplies. How nice a facility do you want and need? What is suitable for your employees? What do you need to convey a proper image to suppliers and customers who are visiting your office? You will need to make these choices at least every two to three years. Because there is significant productivity loss every time you move, try to make facilities decisions that can scale at a reasonable level over a two-year period.

Even if you outsource on the administrative side, you will have bookkeeping, accounting, legal, finance, insurance and compliance costs. Making decisions in this area not only requires you to choose between "make" and "buy," but it is also about productivity and teamwork. I would much rather spend a little more on a highly competent and experienced attorney than to have someone for less who is still green. The cost of doing something wrong can be catastrophic for a startup.

(3) Product Development

In addition to people costs for product development, there can be significant costs for lab equipment, tools, and processes. Some of these are hard costs, while others are soft costs. In an engineering or scientific organization, hard costs might include workstations, oscilloscopes, scanning electron microscopes, and wet lab equipment. However, without the right training, processes and procedures, you can incur high costs in time and quality – sometimes causing you to have to redo things over and over. You absolutely want to avoid this. Time to market, speed of decision-making, and efficiency are some of a startup's best weapons. Big companies have more money, more talented people and more resources than you, so you need to be speedy, nimble, and efficient; otherwise, it is extremely difficult to win. Develop an MVP if possible to gain early target customer feedback in real usage situations.

(4) Operations & Manufacturing

Once you have and are shipping a product, you will need to manage a supply chain and vendors. You will have inventory, accounts receivable, accounts payable, credit & collections, and management control systems to ensure that things are done correctly, legally, and with integrity. If you are making a product that will ship in massive unit volumes, you will need to instill quality control systems that will prevent you from throwing away large amounts of money – or even worse, shipping a defective product to your customers.

Another thing that's important to some startups – especially if you have to build factories or there are large equipment outlays – is **capital requirements**. If you have a manufacturing operation, you will have the cost of the plant, property and equipment. These businesses are typically called **capital intensive**, because you buy a lot of things that are capitalized on the balance sheet and expensed over time based on the useful life of the capital item. **Capital** is the stuff you buy that lasts longer – for example, big servers, a manufacturing facility, or even office equipment. From an accounting standpoint, you do not fully expense capital assets in the period that you purchase them. You will typically capitalize these assets (i.e., put that on the balance sheet) and amortize or depreciate them over a time that represents the useful life of the asset, typically three or five years.

Let's say you spend $150 buying a new piece of equipment with a three-year amortization. You would only expense $50 of that expense in the first year, assuming you have straight-line depreciation, $50 in the second year, and $50 in the third year. If you have very large capital requirements, it's very important to explain to investors your total capital requirements and why you need to make these investments. Your cash requirements to support capital expenditures are an important part of your overall business model. Even though you are only going to expense $50 per year of that $150 expenditure, you are going to spend all $150 in cash when you buy the equipment.

If you are going to raise outside capital from institutional investors, it is essential that you get the accounting right, and you get your financial statements audited by a reputable accounting firm.

If you have the opportunity to lease equipment, you can do that cost effectively, or you can buy used or secondhand equipment. That can sometimes help lower your capital requirements. However, if you have a capital-intensive business, it's crucial to outline why you are going to need those things in your business plan.

(5) Marketing & Sales

Marketing is about understanding markets, defining target customers, building brand awareness, generating customer interest, generating sales leads and driving product strategy and competitive positioning. As such, marketing department members are tasked with understanding your customers in the context of the target market you are serving. This group also provides the tools and training necessary to make products easier for customers to use, and easier for salespeople to sell. Some of the functions that marketing should manage are public relations, communications, advertising, and brand management. In today's online world, you also need to have a digital marketing strategy that includes a killer website and content marketing. Ultimately, the key role of the marketing department is to drive lead generation in the target product-market segment, and help to win customers.

The sales function is complementary to marketing with a more direct focus on managing customer relationships, driving action, lead conversion and closing sales. Implicit in this is a customer service component, which usually includes travel and entertainment expenses. When you combine marketing and sales expenses, you can see that the overall cost of sales is a significant and frequently overlooked cost in a startup. Most investors will be just as interested in your customer engagement strategy, your customer acquisition costs, and the total value of a customer as they are in your product.

(6) Fundraising

In a startup, keeping "gas in the tank" is a crucial part of the CEO and CFO's job descriptions. Without fuel, it is not possible to launch a rocket; without adequate capital, it is hard to build a startup from an idea into a product, and eventually into a company. The direct costs of raising money include travel and management time. However, this is an area of expenses where there can be massive efficiency and productivity loss, as well as opportunity cost. Having a "captain at the helm" who knows how to balance the operational challenges of building and running a company with the challenges of keeping a flow of money to execute the plan is critical for any startup. Fundraising is a frequently overlooked and misunderstood area – and quite often, the cause of many startups' ultimate demise.

(7) Decision Making

As mentioned earlier, speed of decision-making is one of the most important weapons a startup has. Since it's not a direct cost, CFOs do not see this as a line-item expense. However, it is one of the most important "costs" in any company, and especially startups. Implicit in decision-making is risk management. It is worth reading the article in *Forbes*, "Decision Making: Tips for First Time Startup CEOs." The idea that "time is money" is universally understood, and it is critically important when it comes to operating a startup. Efficiently and productively making good decisions is essential for startup success. Time to market and time to revenue are both essential metrics for startups. While running a big company is akin to driving across the country, running a startup is more like launching an F-16 fighter plane from an aircraft carrier. You only have a limited runway, so you better use it properly and get the plane in the air instead of in the ocean!

Leadership and management are significant components of decision-making. As a company founder, you need to accurately and clinically assess your own skill set versus the company's needs. You should surround yourself with capable mentors and advisers who can give you guidance based on experience and expertise, not just theory. You may also need to make a decision at some point to bring an outside CEO or executive into the company that can help get you to "the next level." These are never easy decisions, but they can sometimes be the difference between success and failure.

The Importance of Cash Flow and Cash Management in a Startup

The next thing to look at is cash flow. You need to understand your monthly burn rate, or the amount of cash you are using monthly, and why there might be large cash outlays at certain times. You should understand your cost per employee, your revenue forecast and its key components for the customer build up.

Cash is king with startups. Since most startups are not generating cash flows, the way you plan to use your cash while you are building your business becomes absolutely critical. Being able to describe your plan for cash usage, what milestones you can expect to achieve, and what investors can expect you to achieve based on this cash usage is very important.

Most of the cash requirements come out of both capital expenses and other expenses. However, as you are ramping up a business, there is also usually a need to account for cash for **working capital** – your company's current assets minus the current liabilities. As you are selling products or services, you are going to have accounts receivable when you have already sold the product – yet have not collected the cash from the customer. You are also going to have inventory. You have to buy the product from your suppliers before selling it to the customers. Those are both considered current assets.

You are going to have some amount of your cash tied up in accounts receivable and in inventory. You will subtract accounts payable from that, because that's cash you have not paid to potential suppliers. In my most recent product company, we needed to carry anywhere from 60 to 90 days of inventory, and our typical payment terms for customers were 45 days. In a business where you *Cash is king with startups.* are ramping production, you can have a lot of cash tied up in working capital. This is partially to offset not paying for suppliers immediately, or carrying an accounts payable balance. However, in the case of startups and young companies, suppliers are less likely to sell to you by extending credit terms, which increases the amount of cash tied up in working capital. Obviously this is a bigger problem with hardware and physical product businesses versus software. It is also a bigger problem with product companies versus service companies.

Sometimes you are not able to get financing terms from your suppliers as a startup. You might be in a less favorable position from a working capital standpoint than a more established company. I have seen many situations where startups had to pay in advance or "as they go." This becomes a bigger issue from a working capital perspective as you are building your business. Keep in mind that you need to account for that in the amount of money you raise for the company.

Many venture capital investors will discount this and tell you that you can easily go out and get a working capital line of credit (e.g., a bank loan secured by your inventory and accounts receivable) when you are building your business. However, that may or may not be the case. Regardless, you need to forecast working capital in your cash needs.

Timing to Break-Even

Your financial model must show a reasonable timeframe for break-even – which occurs when your operating expenses are less than or equal to your company's gross margin or contribution margin. In any business, you ultimately need to get to a point where you are paying your own bills. Then, ideally, as you drive profitability you will experience **operating leverage** over time. This is where the profits grow faster than the expenses, and where you can show that you have a scalable business model.

People need to see this to truly believe that they are going to be able to make money on your business. To reiterate: having explosive revenue growth with healthy gross margins is the most important thing for most venture investors. They want to see a large market that's growing fast, where you have a dominant position. Some might give you some grace and believe that operating leverage will exist. However, a more sophisticated investor might ask more questions around this and focus a little more on the profits, and not just on revenue growth.

Customer Acquisition Costs (CAC) and Lifetime Value of a Customer (LTV)

Investors are dialing more deeply into a couple of critical marketing and sales expenses these days. Specifically, they will probably look more closely at your customer acquisition cost (CAC) – that is, how much money you need to bring a new customer on board. This will help them to assess the cost of a customer diversification plan. They are also considering the Customer's Lifetime Value (LTV). If an average customer purchases $1,000 of your products every month, on average, and you keep customers for five years, on average, then the average LTV is $60,000 ($1,000 X 12 months X 5 years). You should understand and articulate these costs and have goals for them. Perhaps you can streamline your sales process and thus reduce your CAC, or maybe you will add additional product lines or services that will increase your LTV.

CAC is not a line item on the P&L, but it's still one of the most important expenses to measure. It consists primarily of marketing and sales expenses. Market research is critically important to startups and growth-stage companies. You will recall that this is part of the situation analysis where you validate the market opportunity by looking at market size, market growth, the competitive landscape, and which critical customers make up your business.

Projecting Market Share

To project market share, you will need to look back at the size and growth of your served available market and the total available market that you came up with in the situation analysis. You will also need to revisit your revenue goals as a percentage of that number. This will help you determine what kind of market share you can expect over time.

If you are the innovator in a whole new product area, you are going to have 100% market share of the SAM out of the gate. Of course there is no way of growing through market share gains in this scenario – so, you have to assume that you are going to lose some market share over time. In most industries that are not completely commoditized, there is one dominant player who maintains somewhere around 65% to 70% market share, even as competition enters the market. There are innumerable examples of this.

The Importance of Milestones

There are key milestones that match up with financial goals, and other milestones that could have a significant financial impact, like winning a major new customer. A purely financial goal is a number, like $1 million in revenue per quarter, or reaching break-even. When you set key milestones, they need to be time bound.

You need to include critical milestones in your financial plan. A good way to think about this is: you have X number of new customers coming on board and generating Y new revenues each year, or each quarter or each month. Showing that from a bottoms-up perspective is very important. You need to have a sales funnel that demonstrates this potential revenue, with clearly identified customer targets. You also need strong market opportunities that exhibit explosive growth.

Yet even in good markets with explosive growth opportunities, it's difficult – if not impossible – to predict exactly when growth ignites. Investors want to see proof of your business model – specifically, what milestones you plan to meet and how that translates into future revenue growth.

Investor Expectations of Financial Knowledge

A CEO needs to understand his or her company's numbers at a high level. Company founders who can credibly describe the business model in both qualitative and quantitative terms convey much more authority with most investors. Some CEOs are purely genius, technical gurus. These individuals might have a strong CFO who works through the numbers; but typically, even those CEOs come across as much more credible if they at least have a working knowledge of the numbers at a high level.

You also need someone on your team who knows your numbers cold, and can speak to them at a deep level. This could be your CFO, your head of finance, or perhaps even your marketing person. Maybe a combination of two of these individuals can help bring a couple of complementary perspectives to the numbers. For example, the CFO might have a great understanding of revenue growth and percentages from a purely financial perspective, and your head of marketing might have a better understanding of the underlying customers that are driving that revenue growth.

If you are raising money, you need to include a funding request and use of funds in your plan. Having a financial plan grounded in reality – and that you can defend – will enhance your believability with potential investors. To come across as knowledgeable, your financial plan has to be validated from both a tops-down and bottoms-up perspective – and it needs to have resiliency. In other words, if you have a 5 to 10 percent increase or decrease in sales volume, selling prices, or product cost, it is important to understand how this affects your overall business model.

Investors also like to see some level of flexibility in CEOs and company founders. You can demonstrate this by your willingness to raise less money right now and have a Plan B that still achieves significant milestones versus the Plan A that might be the "swing for the fences" type of plan. Investors might still want to go for the "swing for the fences" Plan A, but they want to know that you can adapt to circumstances. Obviously, conditions change over time – and having someone that they can work with when the going gets tough, and who can be a little more frugal and a little more creative, becomes very important.

Return on Investment – ROI

Investors are interested in return on investment and Internal Rate of Return, or IRR. While these aren't explicitly called out in your financial goals and plan, you need to understand that investors will be evaluating your business model based on these metrics.

Understanding the potential ROI and IRR for your business is important. Investors need to find firms or companies to invest in that have an ROI of at least 10X. The real winners deliver much more than that, 50X or 100X. The best performing companies in a venture portfolio typically do what investors call "return the fund." That is, if they have a $200 million fund, the investment made in your company returns $200 million to their fund. If investors only own 10% of the company, that company needs to have a $2 billion market cap in order for the numbers to work.

If a company is not going to be worth at least a billion dollars on exit, it's difficult for the largest and most prominent venture capital firms to invest in your company. A more modest exit might be acceptable for other types of investors, but you still need to have a company that is addressing a large, rapidly growing market with the chance to deliver spectacular returns.

In general, venture capitalists have moved pretty far "upstream" in the private company investing process to reduce risk and gain more certain returns. In other words, they are primarily focused on growth stage investments, typically Series B and Series C financing rounds, with some limited consideration for a Series A financing. They are not as frequently funding Seed capital deals. Outside Silicon Valley, it's even less likely for the top VC firms to be involved at a Seed or even Series A stage. Part of the reason for this trend is that most of these VCs want to see additional proof-points of the validity of a company's business model before making an investment. This includes scaling of revenue at a reasonable level and proof that the product works in the target customer's environment.

Hopefully by this point in your growth, some of the technology and initial market risks are gone – and you are enjoying market expansion while growing and acquiring additional customers. VC firms are more likely to be involved when your overall business model has some reasonable level of scale and market validation.

How Much Money Should You Raise?

The answer to "How much capital should I raise?" depends on two key factors: how much money you need to achieve your next set of key milestones and how much capital is available to your firm. In other words, you may need to ratchet up or ratchet down your expectations depending upon what your current opportunity is and the progress that you have made.

How much progress has been made in your product development? Do you have initial customers? Are those customers ramping to production volumes? Have you validated your solution with more than one customer, and are you now diversifying your customer base? Have you met the key milestones you have discussed with prospective investors to grow your credibility with them? Answers to these questions will give some indication what stage of investment you should be seeking.

The reasonable amount of capital available to your startup depends entirely upon the ROI and investor confidence. These elements are grounded in your company's perceived market size and growth, which translates into revenue potential. Your unique value proposition and sustained competitive advantage translates into your market share, and target customer perception of the value of your solution translates into your gross margin.

You can see how the qualitative and quantitative elements of a strategic plan, and ultimately a business plan, tie together – and directly result in how much money you can raise for your startup.

We've talked through a lot of specific financial terms and processes in this chapter, but the most important steps are to establish financial goals in the strategic planning process. Once you have a clearly defined road map, those financial goals translate into a financial plan that's part of your business plan. You need to balance revenue projections between tops-down, which is market related, and bottoms-up, which is sales funnel related - and they must be reasonable. You must track the financial metrics that are important to your startup. These are the dials on the machine that you need to be able to tune up or tune down - the biggest of which is, obviously, your cash burn rate.

Outside investors focus on ROI and IRR, so you need to understand what those are and how they translate into your business. Your plan should consider that there is a reasonable amount of capital available for your company – and keep in mind that what is reasonable depends on your market opportunity. Most companies in any type of outside institutional round are typically going to give up anywhere from 15% to 25% of their company for whatever amount is invested. What valuation you have "pre-money" will significantly affect how much money you raise.

Depending upon how much money you need to raise and where you are in the cycle of your growth, you will be reasonably attractive to certain investors, including Angel investors and venture capitalists. However, there are also other sources of funds these days, including equity crowdfunding, which might be the right solution for you.

Crowdfunding and the U.S. JOBS Act

In the old days, when a startup wanted to raise startup equity financing for their company, and they had exhausted their own funds and money from friends and family, they would look to Angel investors and eventually to venture capital firms.

Although this is still a very viable method for funding your startup, with the passage and implementation of Title II, III, and IV of the U.S. JOBS Act, there are now a few alternatives for raising outside capital for your startup. This section is intended to give an overview of the four types of equity funding available to startups, before taking a company public in an Initial Public Offering, or IPO.

Rule 506(b) of Regulation D

This law allows small businesses to raise an unlimited amount of startup equity financing from an unlimited number of accredited investors. Rule 506 of Regulation D is considered a "safe harbor" for the private offering exemption of Section 4(a)(2) of the Securities Act of 1933. Companies relying on the Rule 506(b) exemption can raise an unlimited amount of money from an unlimited number of "accredited investors" and up to 35 other non-accredited investors. An accredited investor, in the context of a natural person, includes anyone who:

- Earned income that exceeded $200,000 (or $300,000 together with a spouse) in each of the prior two years, and reasonably expects the same for the current year, *OR*
- Has a net worth over $1 million, either alone or together with a spouse (excluding the value of the person's primary residence)

The company cannot use general solicitation or advertising to market the securities. Under Rule 506(b), a company can ensure it is within the Section 4(a)(2) exemption by satisfying the following standards:

- Unlike Rule 505 of the Securities Act, all non-accredited investors, either alone or with a purchaser representative, must be sophisticated – that is, they must have sufficient knowledge and experience in financial and business matters to make them capable of evaluating the merits and risks of the prospective investment.
- Companies must decide what information to give to accredited investors, so long as it does not violate the anti-fraud prohibitions of the federal securities laws, but companies must give non-accredited investors disclosure documents that are generally the same as those used in registered offerings.
- If a company provides information to accredited investors, it must make this information available to non-accredited investors as well.
- The company must be available to answer questions by prospective purchasers, and financial statement requirements are the same as for Rule 505 of the Securities Act.

Purchasers of securities offered pursuant to Rule 506 receive "restricted" securities, meaning that the securities cannot be sold for at least a year without registering them.

Reg D offerings are the traditional way that private companies raise money from Angel investors, which by definition are accredited investors. Private placements of preferred stock to venture capital funds and corporate investors are also issued as unregistered shares with restrictions under Reg D. There are also some more limited forms of Reg D offerings including 504 and 505 offerings.

JOBS Act Title II

Title II of the U.S. JOBS Act allows businesses to publicly advertise their need for startup equity financing. The new exemption it created, Rule 506(c), lifted the ban on general solicitation that was adopted in 1933. Companies can now raise an unlimited amount of capital from an unlimited number of accredited investors.

Under Rule 506(c), a company can broadly solicit and generally advertise the offering, but still be deemed to be undertaking a private offering within Section 4(a)(2) if:

- The investors in the offering are all accredited investors; and
- The company has taken reasonable steps to verify that its investors are accredited investors, which could include reviewing documentation, such as W-2s, tax returns, bank and brokerage statements, credit reports and the like.

Purchasers of securities offered pursuant to Rule 506 receive "restricted" securities, meaning that the securities cannot be sold for at least a year without registering them.

Title II has allowed for syndicated Angel deals using online platforms like Angel.co.

JOBS Act Title III

Title III of the U.S. JOBS Act allows for non-accredited investors to invest in private startup companies. Title III of the JOBS Act, otherwise known as Regulation Crowdfunding or Reg CF, legalized retail investment crowdfunding. In other words, non-accredited investors can now participate broadly in this type of startup equity financing. There is a good list from CrowdFund Insider that outlines what issuers, or those looking to raise funds, should know about Title III. I have included it here:

- You may only raise $1M in a rolling 12-month period
- You must use an online intermediary
- You must be a U.S. entity
- You must disclose certain financial information, and depending on how much you plan to raise, your financial statements may need to be reviewed or audited by an accountant
- You must fulfill certain ongoing reporting requirements
- You may raise funds from both accredited and non-accredited investors, although investors are limited to investing a certain dollar amount based on their income or net worth.

Title III went into effect in May of 2016. It allows for "retail" non-accredited investors to invest in private companies.

Regulation A+ of Title IV of the JOBS Act

Reg A+ is a type of offering which allows private companies to raise up to $50 million in startup equity financing. Like an IPO, Reg A+ allows a company to offer shares to the general public and not just accredited investors. Companies looking to raise capital via Reg A+ will first need to file with the SEC and get approval. The fees associated with a Reg A+ offering are much lower than a traditional IPO, and the ongoing disclosure requirements are much less burdensome, and less expensive. Currently there is not a mainstream market for trading shares of stock issued in a Reg A+ offering. This is a major distinction from shares that are offered in an IPO on the NYSE, NASDAQ, or a secondary exchange.

Reg A+ opens up the market for "retail" non-accredited investors to invest in private companies even when they are raising large amounts of capital, without the company going through an IPO.

More than ever before, there are many innovative and creative ways to fund your startup. Pick the alternative that is right for you and your company. If you plan to raise startup equity financing, no matter what path you take, make sure that you have a competent corporate attorney who understands securities law as it relates to startups, mergers & acquisitions, and public financing.

Now let's take a look at your goals over the next three years. Where do you want to take your product and company over that period of time? This is the Winner's Solution of the strategic plan.

CHAPTER 6

Focus on the Destination

Although ideation is the beginning of creating your product or service, you need to take some additional steps to make that idea into a successful business. Your destination – or more accurately, destinations – from a total product standpoint, is what we call the winner's solution of the strategic planning process. In other words: your solution is more than just the product itself. There are other complementary components in addition to the actual product or service that you sell. These other components of the **total product** are essential for you to win in the marketplace and beat the competition.

You'll recall that the most significant elements of your idea are its **unique value proposition** and **sustainable competitive advantage**. A unique value proposition requires that you understand your customers' business problems as well as you understand your own solutions. This allows you to translate from your technical jargon into terms that your customers can understand. You need to speak your customer's language, and see things from their perspective. This doesn't mean trying to teach the customers about their own business – which is an ineffective approach, and very upsetting to nearly all customers. This is about understanding, empathy, and speaking in terms of customer problems first, then your solution second.

Figure 6.1 - Strategic Planning Process - Winner's Solution

Sustaining a competitive advantage as it relates to specific product features is something of a myth. According to a research study found in "Competitive Advantage and the Basis of Competition" by Philip Birnbaum and Andrew Weiss, from the University of Southern California Center for Effective Organizations, today's competitive advantage becomes tomorrow's basis of competition. That is – whatever "special feature" you have this year, everyone else in your industry will have next year. Product features that are essential for even being considered a viable source to your target customers are considered the **basis of competition**. In other words, all competitors have these features. This is sometimes called "table stakes," an analogy from the world of poker.

Figure 6.2 - Dissipation of a Competitive Advantage

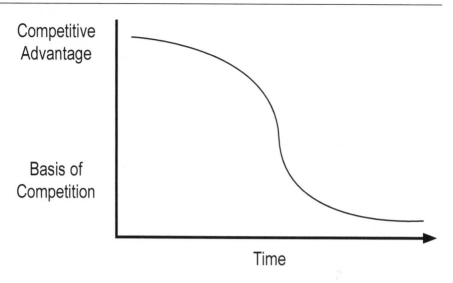

Sustaining a competitive advantage truly requires that you come up with new competitive advantages over time and ultimately build layers of competitive advantage, which is described below. You do this through creating successive iterations of your total product, incorporating customer feedback, innovating new features and capabilities, and having a strong product roadmap.

You do not want to be a one-trick pony. You cannot sustain success by offering a solution that wins the first-generation design – then have your competition come along with a more cost effective solution in the second generation. That will not build a long-term value proposition for your company. This is what is meant by the phrase, "I do not want to be a pioneer, because they have all the arrows in their back." This phenomenon happens when the **first-mover** establishes the market, and the later entrants to the market reap most of the benefits of the market expansion. This happens if you have a point solution without an evolving roadmap based on customer feedback and marketplace learning, or sometimes if you are too early to the market and a fast follower enters the market with a superior product and better market timing. A classic example of this is from the world of internet search: in 1998 goto.com, a small startup later renamed Overture, created the Pay Per Click (PPC) search engine and advertising system, and demonstrated it at a TED conference. It was not until October 2000 that Google offered its version of a PPC advertising system called AdWords, allowing advertisers to create text ads for placement on the Google search engine. In 2003, Overture was acquired by Yahoo for $1.6 billion. Fast forward to 2016: Google ad revenue was about $20 billion per quarter. At the beginning of 2017 the global market share in online search was:

- Google: 80.5%
- Bing (Microsoft): 6.9%
- Baidu: 5.9%
- Yahoo: 5.4%

You can see from this example that the first-mover was not the ultimate winner in the internet search business, by a long shot. In the Harvard Business Review article, "The Half-Truth of First-Mover Advantage," the authors identify two factors that powerfully influence a first mover's fate:

1. The pace at which the **technology of the product in question is evolving** and
2. The pace at which the **market for that product is expanding**.

In other words, there are structural reasons why a first-mover advantage can exist. However, even if that structure exists, you need to continue to innovate, build barriers to entry, and create other layers of competitive advantage. Generally, being the first mover is a big advantage in most technology and life science-based companies. However, in some cases it is better to be a fast follower than to be a first mover, as discussed above.

You may find in discussions with customers that your solution has a strong competitive advantage in generation one. However, as you get to generations two, three or four, you need to incorporate feedback from the customer into your **Total Product Concept**.

The Total Product Concept

Let's talk about the total product description. When you are selling a product to a customer – especially if it's a more sophisticated technical product – you are selling more than just the product itself. In other words, there are other complimentary components in addition to the actual product or service that you sell. This is the **total product concept**.

Figure 6.3 - Total Product Description

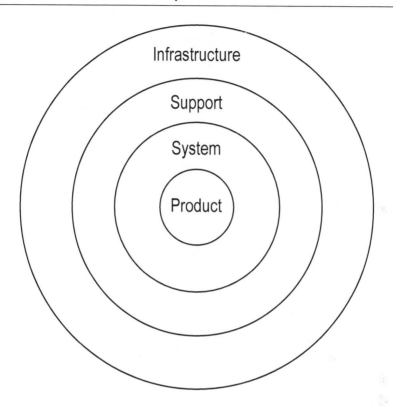

This figure shows a series of concentric circles with the basic product that's sold to the customer at the core. This is what you actually sell, and how you generate revenue. The core product includes price, warranties, delivery dates, packaging, any essential updates, and any product revisions that are supplied to customers.

Layered on top of that, you typically have a system. This is a product commercialization model, including your go-to-market plan, branding, promotion, and other marketing activities. It includes your customer support model, or the set of things you do that customers require or desire in support of your product. Support includes what you provide in the initial usage and what ongoing support you need to provide over time. This does not just apply to large corporations operating in a B2B environment.

For example, it is very common for freelance website designers to have an ongoing service contract to maintain the site and ensure quality operation. Another example is companies that install home networking and home security systems, which frequently offer ongoing service agreements and monitoring. The system may also include third-party products that are typically sold with your products. These might be items that your ecosystem partners supply, and you need to ensure that your product works in conjunction and harmony with third-party products. A good example of this is the ecosystem of third party applications available on both Apple and Android-based mobile devices.

Layered on top of that is additional support by your sales channels, which you might divide by market segment. Maybe you have a different set of sales channels or value-added resellers for different end customers. You have to tie that in with the system model. These things interact with each other. If these channels are distributors or value-added resellers, also known as VARs, then they may also supply some of the third-party products.

Finally, you have infrastructure: the systems and processes that you use to track and drive sales of your products. It could be sales funnel tools, your online platform, and your partner ecosystem. It also includes the human and personal relationships that you need in order to define and develop additional products in your roadmap.

These concentric circles combined make up the total value proposition of your total solution. You need to have a clear picture of that in your winner's solution for years one, two, and three of the strategic plan as part of your comprehensive product roadmap.

Layers of Competitive Advantage

The research shows that having just a single competitive advantage will not last a very long time – even if you are protecting it with intellectual property. This is where the concept of layers of competitive advantage over time comes in.

Inevitably, the customer will ask you, "What have you done for me lately?" As such, you need to build other commercial things into your solution that creates barriers to entry for the competition. Can you closely marry your product to your customers' products to build in switching costs?

Figure 6.3 - Total Product Description

Superior Price Performance

Superior Service & Quality

Best Maintenance & Roadmap

Build Switching Costs

Protection of Intellectual Property

Product Unique Value Proposition

It is not uncommon in technology platform products to have the customer's software or customization tightly integrated with the product you are selling. If customers are used to the way they use your product and have to learn something new if they move to a competitor, they are more likely to stick with you. Even if the competitor has comparable quality and price performance, if it's significantly costly for the customer to move from your solution to your competitor's solution, this gives you time to work through things and make sure that you have the sustained advantage there.

A point solution will never give you a sustainable competitive advantage over time; you need a strong **roadmap of follow-on products and features**. It is also important that you continue to evolve your ecosystem, and leverage your solutions into adjacent markets over time.

Your new and improved solution may not be a breakthrough innovation. However, you will sustain an advantage over time if you continue to evolve your product – especially if you do a good job of protecting your intellectual property. When the development cost of the customer is not as high because you are leveraging off existing solutions, you achieve something we call "backward compatibility" in the tech world. However, it can apply to other types of products as well.

Providing excellent service and quality are also important differentiators. Service and quality may seem subtle and hard to measure, but there are ways to quantify them. Great companies define the most important aspects of service and quality for key customers, measure the delivery, and work to constantly improve.

Have you ever heard of "**total value letter**"? This is a letter or memo that you send to your largest and most important customers about all the things that you have done for them in the most recent period. I am a big proponent of using total value letters, and other forms of documentation and communication with key customers. Customers in a B2B environment will often hold quarterly business reviews to drive an agenda with their key suppliers. It is important that you also do these updates with your key customers proactively. Even if you experienced a significant problem with a customer, it is important to describe how you handled the issue and resolved it.

> *To build brand loyalty with your customers, you need to deliver a consistent stream of total products that meet the evolving needs of your customers.*

As competition comes into your market, customers might have exposure to a lower-cost solution. You may not need to match the price exactly, but you need to focus on delivering better **price-performance** – that is, equivalent performance at a lower price, or superior performance at a higher but acceptable price.

To build brand loyalty with your customers, you need to deliver a consistent stream of total products that meet the evolving needs of your customers.

Product Development Cycles and the Sales Cycle in a Multi-Product Situation

Recall from the prior chapter that when generating new products, you must understand the cadence of both your product development engine and your customers' design-in cycle. How long does it take you to develop and launch a new product? This is called your **product development cycle**, and it may be different for different products and different types of products, as we will discuss below in Product Development Mapping. In addition to your product development cycle, you also need to understand how long it takes for a customer to move through your sales funnel, or the **sales cycle**. The sales cycle can also be different lengths of time depending upon the type of product, as we discuss below in Product Development Mapping. More complex products, or new platform products, sometimes have a longer sales cycle, whereas a simple derivative product might be qualified much more quickly. For example, in the automotive industry you would need to start the qualification process for a new platform component in 2017 in order for it to ship in 2021 model-year cars.

Typically, the product development cycle and the sales cycle operate in series – in other words you need to finish the product development before a customer is willing to evaluate your product. Under any circumstance you need to have a product that is at a **sufficient level of maturity** for customers to begin to evaluate it. In many B2B situations, your target customers will have their own product plans that you will need to intersect, or their own budget cycle that you will need to intersect in order to sell your product. If you do not hit this target, and the proverbial "window" closes, you will need to wait for the next window to open before your product can be evaluated. The syncing of your product development and the customer's sales cycle will allow you to establish key **landing zones** for new products that will ramp to production and accelerate time to revenue, assuming you hit those landing zones. A landing zone for your product is a specific date or window that you must hit with your product schedule and feature set to intersect your customers' product development plans, launch cycle, and budget constraints.

Product Development Mapping

As you move beyond a single product strategy and start to diversify your product line and expand into adjacent market segments, you will need to make trade-offs and scope multiple projects simultaneously. At this point, you need to map your development projects. An article in the Harvard Business Review, "Creating Project Plans to Focus Product Development," by Steven C. Wheelwright and Kim B. Clark, describes five types of product development that vary in scope and complexity. They are:

- Breakthrough Projects
- Platform Projects
- Derivative Projects
- Research and Development (R&D) Projects
- Alliance and Partnership Projects

The product development tool provides a great framework for scoping the amount of resources and time it will take to complete different types of development projects. Even if you have a very experienced product development leader, this tool is still a great way to have a dialogue to determine if the project has been scoped and resourced properly. A frequent problem of startup companies as they reach the growth and product diversification phase is an inability to properly scope and resource projects. This leads to failure in execution, disappointed customers, and sometimes failed businesses and companies. The product development mapping tool allows you to scope things more accurately and assist in making trade-offs that will increase your chances of meeting specific customer landing zones, and

A frequent problem of startup companies as they reach the growth and product diversification phase is an inability to properly scope and resource projects.

ultimately being successful. It is also important to develop platform products that can result in multiple derivatives without having to completely re-architect and re-design the product. In almost any software or hardware project it is important to think about re-use from the beginning of the program, but this thought process can also apply to anything where you have a standard product that requires some type of customization for different customers or different market segments. Consumer products can also follow these same principles.

In the semiconductor chip industry, for example, it may take 24 to 36 months from the start of the project to a commercial product launch – for a breakthrough product where you have to develop everything from scratch. A platform project typically takes 12 to 18 months, and a derivative can be as quick as six months. In addition to the timeline, breakthroughs, platforms, and derivatives all take a different number of resources and mix of resources. Like any industry, you do not want to develop breakthroughs unless you have an opportunity to open up a massive new market opportunity.

Breakthrough Projects bear a lot of risk; so much so that more established companies typically do not tackle them. Their existing customers usually cannot wait that long for a new product cycle. As such, bigger brands typically stick with new platform development and derivatives. Clayton Christensen discusses this situation in his book, *The Innovator's Dilemma*. If an established company does not develop new platforms that result in a number of quick derivatives, they risk failure. They should even design a breakthrough product for re-use so that they can deliver a product roadmap that meets their customer's requirements. In other words – if done right, a breakthrough project is a kind of "super-platform."

Something to keep in mind if you are one of the many startups developing a new breakthrough product is that you should be shooting for a 10X improvement in price-performance over existing solutions in the market. It is important that your product has intermediate milestones that validate the value of your solution. This could be a demonstration, a prototype, or an MVP, a minimum viable product, as described in the last chapter.

In some technology, life science and biotech industries, it can take three to five years from the initial idea to product commercialization for a new breakthrough. If you do not have any intermediate milestones to validate the product-market opportunity, then you will have a difficult time getting investors interested in your company. If you are fortunate enough to secure your initial outside investors, it's still a challenge to get subsequent rounds of financing that give step-ups in valuation under these circumstances.

Platform Projects have less significant changes in both the product and processes as compared to a breakthrough. **Derivative Projects** are derived from a platform. As you might expect, breakthrough projects take more time and resources than platform projects, and platforms take more time than derivatives. However, if you do not create platforms, then you will never have derivatives. In other words, if you do not create platforms, then it is likely that you will never get any leverage in your product development efforts and the associated operating leverage from a financial perspective. Also, you will never benefit from the rapid creation of derivatives. Bottom-line: Implement a platform strategy in your product development projects.

You may also need to develop building block technologies for these products. These are called **R&D Projects**. Although these projects have significant changes in both the product and process similar to a breakthrough project, they are very focused projects to develop key **"building blocks"**

Implement a platform strategy in your product development projects.

versus a fully commercialized product. Therefore, you do not need a full product team on these projects. An innovative technology that you can use and leverage across multiple products is in the R&D Project category. In this case, you need to develop and validate the core technology as a building-block technology first, then incorporate that building block into actual products. The successful development of these core technologies bears such a high risk that it is too risky, even for a startup, to incorporate these capabilities into a full product without validating them as a stand-alone technology first. Examples of R&D Projects from my experience are development of a new high-performance radio-frequency technology in an unproved process technology, and the development of a new type of transistor cell on an unproved material.

You can also execute on **Alliances and Partnership Projects**. Small startups are usually not doing more than one or two main projects at a time. If your first project is not in the platform or breakthrough category, you're not likely to have a very valuable startup company. You need to have a platform where you can get multiple derivatives – or a breakthrough where you can derive at least one or two platforms that can get derivatives out of those. That's how you leverage your R&D dollar, and get re-use. That needs to be comprehended in the initial product.

You need to have a partner ecosystem in almost all complex products. These strategic partnerships will be critically important to your overall strategy. Identify your core competencies and areas where you are going to deliver products and solutions. Then, build an ecosystem around this core that allows you to outsource the rest of the solution from world-class partners in their area of specialization that is outside your core competencies. Partners can provide complementary capabilities to create an excellent total product. No company can do it all themselves, including large companies like Apple and Cisco. They have partners. Recall the concentric circles of Total Product concept.

Generating Customer Awareness and Demand

Of course, in order to reach customers, you need to generate customer awareness. Even the most fantastic solution is useless if your customers do not know you have it. That means you have to use a combination of traditional advertising with traditional media and social media.

Any company today needs a killer website that comprehends search engine optimization so that your company can be found by people searching for topics that are relevant to your areas of specialization. You need to have a digital and content marketing strategy in addition to traditional marketing, which should include contributed articles and blog posts. You need to have testimonials and case studies for traditional media and trade press, as well as for your website and to integrate with your social marketing strategy. You need to have press releases; but you need to leverage those through social media. You need thought leaders to help promote your brand.

To generate revenue, look at your company from a tops-down, market-driven standpoint – and balance that with a bottoms-up, customer-driven standpoint. Identify key customers that can help you meet that part of the objective, and realize that bottoms-up support is essential for your first year of revenue. While this really depends on your sales cycle, any business that has not already spoken to or had any intimate involvement with customers will not be able to generate revenue within the next 12 months. Recall that in the prior chapter on financial goals, we went through a detailed explanation of revenue forecasts. We emphasized how a bottoms-up revenue forecast depends upon your product development cycle and your sales cycle.

You need to listen to your customers in defining the winner's solution. However, keep in mind that they may be requesting what they need today – and if takes you 12 to 18 months to develop a new product, then you will show up with something that the customer needed last year instead of what they need now. You are shooting at a moving target when developing new products – so you need to shoot ahead of the target.

Keep in mind that they may be requesting what they need today – and if takes you 12 to 18 months to develop a new product, then you will show up with something that the customer needed last year instead of what they need now.

Focus on your sustainable competitive advantage over time and momentum for revenue growth. You might have a very good bottoms-up plan for the first 12 or 18 months of revenue; however, your three-year plan should be focused more on tops-down and on winning thought leaders and key anchor tenants as customers. If you can acquire customers that are leaders in your business, then others will follow.

A winner's solution must have a unique value proposition and solve critical customer problems. Your company will only remain competitive by building layers of competitive advantage, and a total product solution that relies on ecosystem partners. The winner's solution will create that ecosystem with world-class partners. The next step is to create brand awareness with both traditional and internet-based approaches. You must understand your sales cycle, your forecasting revenue, and have a sales pipeline that makes sense and can be validated. You need to understand your product's development time and life cycle to create a winning and compelling product roadmap.

Now that you have your Financial Goals and your Winner's Solution you can see if you can accomplish everything you desire within the allotted timeframe. Since most startups do not have unlimited resources and unlimited access to capital, this Gap Analysis followed by Gap Resolution is critical. We discuss that in the next chapter.

CHAPTER 7

Necessary Resources to Succeed

Once you have your financial goals and your winner's solution, you need to identify and resolve gaps by undertaking the Gap Analysis and Gap Resolution parts of the strategic planning process. If you are like most companies, you will have more opportunities that you would like to pursue, or a broader set of products or features that you would like to develop, in a finite time. You likely will not have sufficient financial or human resources to do everything that you would like to do. Therefore, you need to narrow your focus. This is what gap analysis and resolution are both about.

By now, you should have completed your situation analysis and the topographical map – so you know where you are today in terms of your markets, customers and competition. You have established your financial goals and the likely financial resources that you will have available over the next one, two and three years. You also have your winner's solution for total product solution, as well as your marketing plans for the next three years. You will be traversing from Point A – the **situation analysis** – to Point B, your **winner's solution**, with the **financial constraints** that you established in your **financial goals**. After you identify and articulate the resources and financial requirements necessary to take this path, you may notice gaps in your available resources.

Figure 7.1 - Strategic Planning Process - Gaps and Plan

You can resolve those gaps by either **resetting expectations or increasing the level of resources necessary to achieve those results**. Many entrepreneurs try to put the proverbial 100 pounds of potatoes into a 50-pound bag. As a startup, you need to do things more efficiently and effectively than big companies, but you need to make trade-offs as well, and get things into real target customers' hands. This may mean that you deliver your product to a narrower customer base, or deliver a more limited feature set in the initial product. The method you choose to make trade-offs between projects and target customers with available resources becomes very important; if you are not careful, this can lead to a downward spiral.

You will typically be developing a single project in an early stage startup, according to the lean startup principles outlined in Chapter 5. The product development map described in Chapter 6 gives a good proxy of your capital requirements to hit your key milestones, whether you have a single product or multiple products. If you only have a single product, but insufficient resources, perhaps you need to develop an initial product with a more limited feature set, and leave the remaining features for your roadmap. This will also help to sanity check what you hear from your development team, and allow you to assess your product design for re-use, manufacturability and scalability. The next big bucket of expenses is marketing and sales, followed by general and administrative, or G&A expenses. These three buckets will determine the amount of funds you need and how you will use them – and investors will be very interested in how you arrived at this number.

Using Zero Based Budgeting, or ZBB, is a common way to resolve gaps between available resources and business goals. However, ZBB has limitations, since it will favor incremental derivative products over breakthrough and platform projects that might be critical for you to establish a new business.

Limitations and Proper Use of ZBB for a Startup

In essence, ZBB is a budgeting method in which all expenses must be justified for each new period. It starts from a "zero base," and you analyze every function within an organization for its needs and costs. You then build budgets around what you need for the upcoming period, regardless of whether the budget is higher or lower than the previous one.

I have encountered some significant limitations to using ZBB in its purest form for any company, but especially for early stage startups. However, this approach does have value, even for startups, for looking at expenses outside of product development – things like marketing, sales, legal, and finance.

When using ZBB to assess product development programs, you look at the overall budget that you are willing to spend, then the expenses associated with each development program. Next you rank-order the development programs by value to the company. Theoretically, the amount of revenue and profits that a project will deliver during the planning cycle is a good proxy; however, this approach has some problems. In a traditional product development process, you only look at the revenue and profits that can be derived from the initial product, even if there is significant re-use available from that product in various derivative products. Thus, there will be a negative bias toward funding platform projects and even more significant negative bias on breakthrough projects. This is a key factor that drives the innovator's dilemma. Startups need to drive breakthrough products that deliver greater than a 10X improvement in price-performance versus alternatives and substitute products on the market. A related issue of using ZBB for breakthrough products is that these projects take more resources, have a longer development cycle, and typically have a longer sales cycle. As such, the revenue from the initial product based on the breakthrough might be outside your three-year planning cycle or even longer. In addition, a significant amount of revenue will be based on derivatives from the breakthrough or platform, and this sometimes is not even considered in baseline revenue projections.

For example, in the development of a breakthrough semiconductor chip it may take 24 to 36 months or more to develop the initial product, and 12 to 18 months to drive any real revenue. Semiconductor chips are an extreme case, like breakthrough biotech cancer drugs. Simpler products like derivatives provide a much quicker return on investment, but must be based on the foundation of a platform or breakthrough project, or they are not even a real derivative; they are simply a point solution that cannot be leveraged from a development standpoint. In this case, there is not any opportunity for re-use, and the product development costs will never get any leverage. This is why the devaluing of breakthroughs and platforms is an inherent limitation to ZBB. I have many examples from my experience, but a classic one is the product roadmap that I inherited at C-Cube Microsystems in their consumer division. A product technology called Video Compact Disk, or VCD, was adopted en masse in China, and C-Cube was the primary technology provider, along with Philips Electronics for VCD. The DVD market had not ignited, but it was clear that DVD would be a worldwide standard and a much larger volume opportunity over time versus VCD. It was likely that DVD would replace VCD even in China. Yet, we had a roadmap with three new VCD products, and one DVD platform product that was on the roadmap to start development in two years. The DVD platform was being neglected for a mature product line. Obviously, my team and I changed the roadmap and resourced the DVD platform. We had to make a case for the long-term viability of the overall business, since ZBB did not result in the right answer. At this point, C-Cube was already a public company, and we almost fell into the trap of the innovator's dilemma.

If you are developing an initial product in the breakthrough or platform category, then you need to establish **product development** as the priority in the company above all other functions. After all – you do not have a company without a product. The next priorities would be the things associated with the total product, including product marketing. The third priority is legal matters – especially legal expenses related the protection of intellectual property. The fourth area of expense prioritization is anything related to product commercialization and sales – legal expenses related to customer contract, development of the sales funnel, your online platform, market channels, and direct sales expenses. You need to have a minimum amount of finance, accounting, and general management expenses.

This takes us to the biggest issue most startup companies face. Assuming you have done a great job in this expense planning, you may still have expenses that exceed your available capital. If you cannot raise sufficient capital to fully resolve the gap, you need to raise sufficient capital to get to **intermediate milestones**. In some cases, there may still be a gap. This is one instance where applying ZBB principles to product development in a target market segment is appropriate and necessary.

For example, I was mentoring an entrepreneur who was developing an online application and cloud-based solution for serving fitness and health professionals. The application supports billing and scheduling of clients, and has a referral engine where fitness and health professionals can refer clients to each other and get a referral fee.

The solution had a traditional desktop and laptop web-based interface, a mobile application, and a cloud-based solution. In the desktop world, you need compatibility with multiple browsers (Firefox, Chrome, Safari, etc.) and two operating systems (e.g., MAC-OS and Windows). The usage of standard web-based interfaces and programming languages, like Hypertext Markup Language, or HTML, solves many of these issues, but there is still real work involved in the development. Mobile platforms include iOS, Android, and Microsoft – each of which requires some unique development and qualification. Some service professionals, like chiropractors, have Health Insurance Portability and Accountability Act, or HIPAA compliance requirements, which affect the product; other service pros like massage therapists and personal trainers have no such requirements. There are also a number of different ways that you can implement each of the major features of billing, scheduling, and referrals – and each of those features has sub-features. Additionally, this company was faced with the choice of how broadly to launch the product geographically. It was a cloud-based product, so they could have launched it nationwide or worldwide. However, service pros typically operate in referral networks that are in the same local geography.

You can easily see that you can make a multitude of choices about what features, vertical markets, and geographic markets to focus on. Focus is key. The riches are in the niches. Everything else becomes part of your product roadmap.

Outside resolving gaps in product development programs versus available resources, the remaining steps of gap analysis and resolution are:

- Identify **critical people and skills gaps** in your team, and plan to hire the right people
- Identify **key partnership gaps** and articulate your plan for filling them
- Identify **production capacity requirements** and **supplier relationships** you need to develop
- Identify **market channel gaps**, and how you are going to fill those

All of these things will give you greater granularity on how you plan to use funds. For example – if you find that you need a senior system engineer or a product marketing manager, you should know how much those people are paid, and base your budgeting on those assumptions.

Assessing Market Attractiveness

Assessing market attractiveness is a great way to "sanity check" the work that you did in the winner's solution and the situation analysis. You might realize during this process that you are developing a winner's solution product that can serve a number of different distinct market segments, or you might be building a product platform that has a number of variants or derivatives that can serve different product-market segments. If you are creating a breakthrough product for a small market that's not very interesting – and you have a weak competitive position – it's probably not a good project. You might have a product that serves a variety of product-market segments, some of which are more attractive than others, either because of the size and growth of the opportunity or the strength of your competitive position. Combining this market tool with the product development map will give you a good idea where your gaps are – and what you need to do to get from point A to point B with a particular product-market segment focus.

The best tool I have found to analyze market attractiveness is the *GE-McKinsey Market Attractiveness Matrix*.

In this tool, when used for a startup or emerging growth company,

Figure 7.2 - GE/McKinsey Matrix

		Business Unit Strength		
		High	Medium	Low
Market Attractiveness	High			
	Medium			
	Low			

Business Unit Strength is really about your competitive position, and industry attractiveness is really about the potential size and growth of your target product-market segments.

Key questions that this matrix tool will help you answer include:

- Are you dealing with an attractive market?
- Is it large or potentially large?
- Is it growing fast or potentially growing fast?
- Will you have a strong competitive position?

These questions will sound familiar, since you answered them in the ideation phase in this book. However, you will have far more data at this stage based on doing a thorough situation analysis and winner's solution. You may have a number of good opportunities, but insufficient resources or money to pursue every one of them all at once. In this case, it is important to pursue the best near-term opportunities first and establish a beachhead where you can have an extremely competitive and compelling solution for that market niche, just like Amazon did by initially focusing on the online sale of books. As you gain stability, size and scale, you can pursue additional segments, since the relative strength of your company and competitive position will improve as you start to establish strong positions in the initial opportunities. Again this is what Amazon did over time by offering many other consumer product categories, like consumer electronics, DVD movies, dietary supplements, and third-party product offerings through the Amazon online platform.

The Output of a Strategic Planning Process: Your Strategic Plan

As we have already discussed, startups initially grow by displacing an inferior solution or by providing something totally new and innovative in a breakthrough market. So you need to know the relative value and absolute value of the target markets that you are pursuing. If you are attacking a highly attractive, rapidly growing market – and you have a strong market position – that's something investors will feel is worth investing in. If the market is relatively small and not growing at all – or even shrinking – and your market position is weak, it's probably not a great market to enter – and investors will see this.

The best place to initially focus as an emerging company is on a **defensible product-market segment** or niche market, where you can carve out a dominant market position. That does not mean the market is extremely niche; but it is not "the whole enchilada," so to speak. Recall Amazon with books, and Facebook with an initial focus on university students. You do not want to start too big – but, your initial breakthrough product needs to have re-use "baked-in" from the beginning. Your R&D dollars must serve to leverage that initial product and intellectual property positions when you are entering new and adjacent product market segments. You should not have to – nor could you afford to – develop breakthrough after breakthrough or platform after platform. You should have scalability built in from the get go, while initially attacking a narrow enough niche and product-market segment that it fits with your available resources and capital plan.

> *Your startup must initially implement a focus strategy. Focus on a narrow enough product-market segment so that you can dominate it, but with a big enough overall opportunity that this can be a big and rapidly growing business over a reasonable amount of time.*

If you want to go after a market that's going to cost you $1 billion to enter, it's probably not a great opportunity for a startup, even if it is a $50 billion market. If you can carve out a defensible niche that costs you $1 million, $2 million or $5 million after product development and marketing, maybe that's something that's very interesting if it can deliver a 10X return on investment.

Your startup must initially implement a focus strategy. Focus on a narrow enough product-market segment so that you can dominate it, but with a big enough overall opportunity that this can be a big and rapidly growing business over a reasonable amount of time. Your primary advantage as a startup is speed – including time-to-market, decision-making flexibility, speed of decision-making, and time to revenue. Remember, the best way to attack a market is to **establish a beachhead** and expand from there. Develop products that **incorporate re-use** so that you can enter **adjacent market segment opportunities**. Make sure that your **platform supports derivatives**, so you can go after those. Focus on projects that **maximize your core competencies**. Implement a strategy that **protects your IP**.

To review – key outcomes of a strategic planning process include the following:

- Detailed description of your customer and their problem
- Explanation of your solution and your product roadmap from a total product standpoint
- Clearly articulated unique value proposition
- Thorough competitive analysis
- Description of your sustainable competitive advantage and plan for layers of competitive advantage
- Outline of your intellectual property protection position & strategy
- Description of your team, explanation of your core competencies, and plans to build and enhance both
- Description of your partnership plans
- Detailed resources and financial plans
- List of key milestones, plan results and key accomplishments to-date
- Articulation of your critical success factors
- Financial plan and budget that can be explained, understood, and defended
- Clear list of your key assumptions
- Brief description of high probability contingency plans

Keep in mind that contingency plans do not need to be abandonment plans. There will be times when you may need to course-correct – and you will need some ideas on how to adapt and modify if there are things that do not go exactly your way. I consider a slight change in product features based on customer feedback a course correction. A change in initial or key customer focus based on traction is another type of course correction. If you make a drastic change in your product or your market segment focus or both, these can be considered more of a pivot. This is the case because you are abandoning a big part of your investment in either product development or marketing and sales. It is always better to make slight adjustments on a frequent basis versus full-scale changes all at once. However, if you do need to pivot, then make the change and do not delay.

Create a business plan and business model that not only makes sense to you and your team, but to key stakeholders, customers, and potential investors. Remember – you may need to adapt how you explain your strategy so that different target audiences get the message in a language that they understand. As you climb the Hierarchy of Raising Capital pyramid, build off that foundation of a strategic plan, and you will be able to climb the pyramid much more quickly – and face fewer issues along the way.

Of course, you will likely still encounter some stumbling blocks. The **PLAN COMMIT WIN Methodology** is not a panacea. Always keep in mind that failures and setbacks can be stepping-stones to your next success. You just have to learn from these things, make adjustments, and remain flexible and adaptable. When you are running a startup or growth-stage company, you are working in an environment with a significant amount of uncertainty and ambiguity – so you will need to stay constantly vigilant.

It's always good to have feedback and control mechanisms in place that tell you where to course-correct along the way. You want to base these on key milestones, or what are sometimes called Key Performance Indicators or KPIs. Some good measurements to consider are:

- Product development milestones
- Progress with customer penetration and expansion
- Performance against your budget
- Progress on building your team, capabilities, and your core competencies

One of the biggest benefits of a strategic planning process is undergoing the process itself. Although the plan is a valuable baseline for an annual operating plan and budget, just getting the management team and key players in the organization thinking strategically can make a big difference. Running a strategic planning process improves decision-making.

Undergoing this process will give you the opportunity to look at the market and customers in a different way than you do in the ordinary course of business. You will get early indicators and the opportunity to "course-correct" where you would otherwise not even see potential problems and

Running a strategic planning process improves decision-making.

pitfalls. It's difficult to step back and look at the big picture when you are in the "weeds" of day-to-day operations, "fire fighting," and engaging with customers. A thorough strategic planning process will give you those views and that perspective.

The **PLAN COMMIT WIN Methodology** uses a strategic planning process with a system for obtaining all the critical data that investors seek from startup companies looking to raise outside capital. The strategic plan is really the foundation for your annual operating plan – your AOP – as well as a business plan that you will use to raise money for your company. In the next chapter we will look at the specifics involved in bringing your plan to life and making it more actionable and measurable. Both of these things are critically important to drive business success and to raise outside capital.

CHAPTER 8

Getting Specific about Your Plan

Now that you've undergone your strategic planning process, you have a detailed total product plan and roadmap, a resource plan, and an understanding of your headcount requirements. You know which core competencies you have, and which you need to build. You have an understanding of the strategic alliances you have and what you need to put in place. You have a set of detailed short-term and intermediate milestones, as well as the ultimate results that you're trying to achieve over the next three years.

Your strategic plan has annual milestones, but you should have more frequent milestones for the first 12 to 18 months of your business plan, and your annual operating plan, or AOP, should also have more granular and frequent milestones. The **PLAN COMMIT WIN *Methodology*** results in a strategic plan that naturally leads into the next step of planning, namely the

Figure 8.1 - Hierarchy for Raising Capital - Business Plan

AOP, the annual financial and headcount budget, and your business plan. Basing this work on the foundation of a strategic plan will allow you to build an annual plan that makes sense – and one that will withstand the scrutiny of outside investors.

Tool for Running the Business:
The Annual Operating Plan and Budget

You typically have quarterly financials in your first year, and possibly the subsequent two years of your strategic plan. However, you ultimately want monthly financials for the AOP, which overlaps with the first year of the strategic plan. That said, it's usually best to revert back to quarterly financials in the business plan that is used for outside investors, since monthly detail is not required for their purposes, and it frequently raises unnecessary questions.

The AOP outlines a specific, month-by-month plan, with key milestones that you will use to manage your business and track progress and key accomplishments. Key components include:

- **Product Line Business Plan(s)**: Derived from the work you did in winner's solution, with any gap resolution.
- **Marketing Milestones & Results Monitors**: Based on the work you did in the winner's solution and financial goals, with any gap resolution.
- **Sales Funnel**: From your work in the financial goals, with any gap resolution and updates based on progress with customers.
- **Product Development Milestones & Monitors**: From winner's solution with gap resolution.
- **Project Plans**: These are detailed plans that outline product development, customer penetration, and other key activities. The product development mapping process described in the last chapter is used to sanity check the product development plans.
- **Monthly Financial Plan (Revenue & Expenses)**: Directly from the financial goals with gap resolution, but with monthly granularity. For expense management, it's wise to have line-item capital and expense budgets, and to have a headcount budget. In companies that use outsourced resources, contractors, or freelancers, it's a good idea to have a line-item budget for these expenses and headcount as well. If you do not, expenses can get out of control very quickly.
- **Budget Action Plan**: This is directly derived from the expense plan, and should be tied to product development and marketing milestones. In other words, if you are behind in hiring, will you be behind in your product development or marketing goals?
- **Staffing Plan**: This is your headcount and hiring plan. I like to track this separate from dollar budgets, and have controls for sign-off of any full-time hires.
- **Contractor Budget Plan**: As mentioned above, you should track this as its own line item if you outsourced some of your resources. If unchecked, many well-meaning managers will use contractors in place of full-time hires. As a stopgap to keep product development moving forward, this is not all bad. However, it can end up delaying the need to bring key resources onboard to build core competencies. Frequently, contractor employees are mercenaries with no skin in the game and no incentive to be productive. They are paid by the hour, typically at a very high rate – so you need to control and monitor this.

- **Feedback & Control Mechanism**: If you have done a good job of planning, then headcount and budget will have a direct correlation to work output and milestone achievement. You need to have some process for measuring progress and communication with the team. Some ideas are to hold weekly staff meetings and monthly operations reviews to discuss key projects and customer progress.
- **Early Warning Process & Corrective Actions**: Part of the weekly staff meeting should be a review of an executive dashboard that tracks progress on key factors that effect critical milestones. I like to use a red/yellow/green system for communication, along with mitigation plans, and the owners of any action items for anything that is not green.

The AOP and annual budget are the tools that you use to run the business. The business plan for investors is a hybrid of the AOP and key elements of the strategic plan. The financial information in the business plan is a hybrid of the annual financial budget, the annual headcount budget, and the financial plan that results from the strategic planning process for years two and three.

Tool for Marketing the Business: The Business Plan

The sole purpose of the business plan that you present to investors is to provide information to get prospective investors to make an investment in your company. When delivering a startup business plan, telling a story is critical. I am not talking about telling a bedtime story, or the most ridiculous piece of fiction or fantasy that I've ever seen – although I have seen plenty of business plans that are no more than fairy tales. In the context of a startup business plan, the story needs to be grounded in a set of key components that all sophisticated investors want to see before making an investment. All of this information should be contained in a business plan, but it needs to be delivered in a way that investors can hear and understand. As I used to say to my team about customers and investors, "Do not make them think too much, it hurts their head."

A crisp and solid startup business plan that holds together under a reasonable amount of scrutiny is one of the best weapons that an entrepreneur has in his or her quiver of arrows to slay investors and gain funding for their startup. If you have a good business idea and a business plan, along with an associated financial model, a solid pitch deck, a clear elevator pitch, confidence as an entrepreneur, and a reasonable amount of humility, you have the essential components for getting your startup funded.

If you look online, there are a variety of different sources of business plan outlines, including the *US Small Business Administration*, *Entrepreneur* and *Forbes* magazines. All of these sources have very similar outlines including an executive summary, a company description, market description, customer analysis, competitive analysis, management team, and a financial plan. This tells you a couple of things. First, investors are used to getting specific information, and second, they

A crisp and solid startup business plan that holds together under a reasonable amount of scrutiny is one of the best weapons that an entrepreneur has in his or her quiver of arrows to slay investors and gain funding for their startup.

like to get this information in a consistent way. This just makes sense. Professional investors are reviewing tens, if not hundreds, of business plans and executive summaries. Do not try to innovate a new startup business plan outline! It will just create anxiety for potential investors. Deliver your business plan to investors in a format and order that includes all the key information they need and expect to hear. By presenting information in a traditional business plan **structure and flow**, you will allow the investors to focus on the **content** in your presentation. You should tell a **big picture story,** and have the presentation follow a **narrative** flow. Don't create a new structure that would force investors to create a new framework for capturing information in addition to listening to your content. The ideal outline for a business plan suitable for investors looks like this:

- Summary of the Opportunity
- Brief Company Description
- Market Analysis
- Target Customer Description & Problem Assessment
- Product Description & Unique Value Proposition
- Customer Acquisition Cost
- Lifetime Value of a Customer
- Marketing Plan
- Simplified Sales Funnel
- Product Development Plan & Roadmap
- Organization & Management
- Key Team Members & Core Competencies
- Financial Status, Plan and Projections
- Key Milestones
- Funding Request and Call-to-Action

The Executive Summary is the "hook" in a good business plan, and you should be able to use it on a stand-alone basis. This does not mean you have to deliver that information in a boring and uninteresting way.

As a result of the strategic planning process and AOP, you will have a clearer understanding of your markets, your target customers and the problem that you are trying to solve for them. You will have a full grasp of your unique value proposition, your customer acquisition cost (CAC), customer's lifetime value (LTV), and your sustainable competitive advantage. In other words, you will have all the source information you need to prepare a solid business plan for investors.

Prospective investors are looking for you to clearly and articulately describe your business plan and business model – in other words, how you make money. They will also be looking at you individually, your credibility, and your track record – including any milestones that you have achieved to-date.

Remember from prior chapters that timing is critical when it comes to entering a new market, building a product, and raising capital. Where the status of your product development intersects the market helps determine how much money you will be able to raise, and which types and stages of investors you should pursue.

Just like customers, investors need to know, like and trust you before they do business with you. They have to believe in you. The more you communicate and then achieve critical milestones; the more you deliver on results; the more you can easily and articulately validate that the competitive situation has materialized the way you projected; and the more clearly you can describe the unique value proposition that your customer feedback has validated; the more credibility you will have with investors.

Investors need to know, like and trust you.

You need to stay laser-focused and dominate a reasonable-sized niche. The mantra to "go big or go home" is typically not the right one for a startup, at least in the beginning. The way you speak about this, even in written communication, will make a big difference to whether you are able to gain outside investment. Additionally, correctly timing your fundraising efforts is critical for valuation and completing a financing round.

Where Do Entrepreneurs Go Wrong?

First, many companies think they have a plan, and what they really have is a loose set of ideas about a business proposition and their idea. They have not done the homework on the customer, the market, and the competition. Implementing the **PLAN COMMIT WIN Methodology** alleviates this issue. An inability to predict the future with 100 percent accuracy should not be an excuse for not having a plan. Your plan will likely go through a set of refinements as your company progresses, and as you gain valuable customer feedback. Lacking a plan is really like having a boat in the ocean without a rudder in the water – you will have no ability to control your direction at all.

Second, entrepreneurs frequently spend 90 percent of their business plan or investor presentation focused on their product, but investors want to spend maybe 20 percent of the time on the company's product, and the other 80 percent on the business and how you make money.

Third, most entrepreneurs do not understand their audience. In dealing with the vast majority of investors, you are really dealing with what I call, "short attention span theater." These guys and gals are extremely busy and bombarded with business plans all day long. In addition, they are conditioned to say "no" to the vast majority of deal opportunities. In order to gain their confidence, you need to have a business plan, executive summary, and an elevator pitch that stands out from the crowd. The way to stand out is to summarize well and tell a meaningful, engaging, and relevant story. Show a compelling business model, and demonstrate that you personally have "the right stuff" and the right team. We will cover more about the investor presentation and elevator pitch in Chapter 11, but let's look more closely at the executive summary of the business plan here.

The Purpose of the Executive Summary

An executive summary of a startup business plan is first and foremost a summary, so you write it last, even though it is the first thing in the startup business plan. Because it's at the beginning of a business plan, I think many new entrepreneurs try to write it first, and it really does not work. It is a summary! You need to have the in-depth understanding of a strategic business planning process, which we will talk about in a bit, to write a good executive summary.

The executive summary is really designed to grab potential investor interest. It highlights the overall strengths of your business, explains where you are today and where you are going. It shows why your business idea will be successful. If you are developing a business that you plan to be funded by either Angel investors or venture capitalists, you need to have a business model that has the potential to deliver a 10X return on investment.

The executive summary also demonstrates that you have done a thorough market analysis, which is critical to investors. "Thorough" means not only that it's there, but also that you have done it with a critical eye. You are not too optimistic or Pollyanna-ish about your business opportunity. At the same time, you still have a belief and passion about it.

The executive summary also clearly explains the customer pain point, the problem that you are solving for customers, the unmet need, your unique value proposition and why you have a sustainable competitive advantage with the value proposition that you are offering.

Your executive summary should tell a meaningful, compelling and relevant story, as should the full startup business plan. A story has a beginning, middle, and an end. The story should start with the problem that you are solving and why it is a big deal. Give the very big picture. You are on a mission to solve that problem. You have a solution that solves this critical problem better than anyone else, and you can do it over a sustained time, even as competition enters the market. The market is big and growing fast, and people do not realize it yet, but a discerning eye can see it emerging. Your solution has incredible value to your target customers, and your business makes money, and a lot of it. There are bigger competitors in your space that will struggle to develop what you have, and it will be critical to them for their businesses going forward.

Key Components of a Rock Solid Executive Summary

Here are the key elements of the executive summary. Be sure to include them, even with the story:

- **Mission Statement**: A description of your idea in the context of the problem that you are solving. It tells what your business is all about, and is typically several sentences to a paragraph.
- **Brief Product Description**: Give information about what your product does for the target customer. You do not need tons of details about how the product works. You should emphasize your intellectual property position and how it is sustainable. You should focus on the product features, benefits and value.
- **Company Information**: When your business was founded, the names and roles of the founders, the key employees, the number of employees and business locations.
- **Growth Highlights**: Include things like monthly or quarterly revenue growth, gross margin expansion, and operating leverage. If you are pre-revenue and pre-product, there is still an opportunity to talk about growth in terms of your target market.
- **Financial Summary**: Key financial information should be presented as graphs, figures, and infographics. Generally, the presentation should be visual where possible, and where it makes sense. As they

say, a picture is worth 1,000 words. If you have a combination of good pictures and graphics, it will make things a lot easier for investors to understand.

- **Summary of your Future Plans**: What are the goals for the business? What are your key milestones? Where do you want to take your business over the next three years? If you are raising money, which you are always doing as a startup CEO, you want to describe the use of funds, and the funding request.

It is also valuable to have a Call-to-Action. What do you want next from your target audience? What action do you want them to take? This does not mean that you leave follow-up actions in the hands of your target investor. You should be responsible for follow-up, and make it clear what you plan to do next, and when you plan to do it. As we discuss in Chapter 11, raising money is a courting process with professional investors.

Know Your Audience and "Speak" to Them in Their Language

It is critically important that you know your audience. Not all prospective investors are the same. Be willing to tailor your executive summary for your audience, at least for the most important target investors. For example, if you are talking to a purely financial investor, you tailor what you are saying to that audience, and likewise with a technical specialist. Different investors may have a different basis of knowledge that they are operating from. The executive summary should keep your target audience in mind.

You already have all the information for the business plan from the strategic planning process and the AOP. Remember, the business plan and the executive summary are marketing documents to help you raise capital for your company. You just need to package the information in a way that is digestible for investors. For investor marketing purposes, your elevator pitch is the first key marketing tool. The next is the executive summary. Third is the overview presentation for investors, and fourth is an in-depth presentation for investors.

Many companies do not even need the business plan in a document. A sufficiently in-depth presentation along with a set of financials and a capitalization table, or cap table, might be enough in some cases.

Preparing a business plan and an executive summary may sound like a lot of paperwork, but in reality, everything you need is already in your strategic plan, your AOP, and your annual budget. I guarantee that by implementing the **PLAN COMMIT WIN Methodology** you will spend vastly less time pursuing investors, since you will have the level of preparation necessary to attract and close the right investors, and complete your funding process more quickly. The key to building credibility with investors and raising outside capital is to have the information and knowledge necessary to run the business, track results, and articulate the business to prospective outside investors. Assuming, of course, that you have a great business model and the right team to execute the plan.

We will talk more about the investor pitch deck and presentation in the final chapter of this book, but let's first look more closely at building a team and the importance of execution. Even if you complete everything else we've discussed, without these two things it is unlikely that you will raise outside capital for your company.

CHAPTER 9

Building a Winning Team

The team is at the center of the **_PLAN COMMIT WIN Methodology._** Any company other than a sole proprietorship needs to have other people. You want to have a team of people surrounding you that are the best that you can get, and the best in their field, if possible.

One of My Favorite Business Team Experiences

In late 2008 – right as we were hitting the worst economic downturn since the Great Depression – I got a panicked call from DirecTV's vice president of engineering. DirecTV was targeted to be one of our largest end customers, and the VP of engineering was our coach and internal champion for helping us to win business with his company. In any business situation, you want to identify and cultivate these relationships that deliver a win-win

Figure 9.1 - Hierarchy for Raising Capital - Team

situation for your company and the customer, and a win-win for you and your coach. We had developed a customer version of our MoCA solution at their request, and it was having reliability issues in some usage cases. It was a dicey situation: our engineers knew these issues would exist, but the DirecTV engineering team had insisted upon this custom solution in order for us to be awarded the business. There was a real risk that DirecTV was going to scrap our solution and commence a deep re-evaluation of all home-networking technologies. This was an unacceptable answer for DirecTV's VP of engineering, who was working closely with his set-top box suppliers – Entropic's direct customers – to deploy a whole-home DVR solution for DirecTV in 2009. He asked me to fly to New York to see his boss, DirecTV's Chief Technology Officer, to see if we could find a way to get the project back on track.

I booked a red-eye flight to New York with my Vice President of business development. Before I left for the airport, I had a detailed discussion with my team about the situation, and an even more in-depth discussion with Entropic's VP of engineering. He had an idea for an alternative solution that would still meet the DirecTV requirements, and resolve the robustness issue in a relatively short time, and keep the project on track for a fall 2009 deployment at DirecTV.

When we arrived in New York the following day, we got a lecture from the CTO about the situation. He knew that his team was partially responsible for it, so he could not be too hard on us, but he still gave us an ear full. I apologized about the situation and let him know that we had a fix that we could fully implement in the next three to four weeks. He committed to keep Entropic in the design if we could meet that schedule and all of DirecTV's requirements.

If we were not able to recover from this setback, it would have had a huge impact on our 2009 business. So I notified my board about the situation and our recovery plan. The board members were already nervous due to the macroeconomic environment, so this news did not help the situation.

With support and commitment from the engineering leadership at DirecTV, we established a project team with representation from both companies. We brainstormed about the potential solution and established a plan and key milestones.

The engineering teams did most of the hard work, and I continued to communicate on a regular basis with DirecTV's senior management about progress on the solution. The Entropic team worked extra long hours during the entire month of December and throughout the holidays, as did many of the DirecTV engineers. We closely tracked progress and results, and would periodically add more or different people to the team who had the skill sets needed to resolve the issues.

It was one of the best team efforts I have ever witnessed. Everyone was motivated and committed to make the improvements happen. Before the International Consumer Electronics Show (CES) in early January, we had completely implemented and shown proof-of-concept for the new solution. DirecTV's engineering team and their management were delighted with how Entropic handled the situation, and with the solution.

Fortunately for Entropic and everyone else involved, we were able to deliver the good news to DirecTV's management and Entropic's board of directors at CES. It was an amazing feeling, despite all the macroeconomic turmoil. DirecTV ended up becoming Entropic's largest end customer, and

Entropic became a key trusted technology supplier to DirecTV. The strength of the DirecTV business was one of the main things that drove Entropic's valuation to greater than $1 billion over the next two years.

Not just any team could have pulled off a feat like this. A lot went into identifying, recruiting, attracting, onboarding, and motivating the team well before we had this crisis situation. So – how did we go about doing this?

Building and Leading Winning Teams:
Identifying, Attracting, Onboarding, and Motivating

How do you identify and attract people like this to your company? Once you get those people on board, how do you make them as effective as possible in the shortest time? What are some of the key components of leading and coaching a stellar team?

Like many business professionals, I like to use sports and war analogies for business situations. Let's take a look at a team that rows crew. In this analogy, everyone on the team is in the same boat – and all have a common goal of moving that boat forward at a rapid speed.

Figure 9.2 - Winning Teams Row Together in the Same Boat

Everyone should be rowing in the same direction with a unified cadence. If you have ever watched this sport in the Olympics, you know how amazing it is. You can see in the image above that everyone in the boat is a rower except for one person: the signal caller, who is – very appropriately – looking forward. He is the guide, and sets the direction and helps with course-correction if necessary.

If only all companies worked like this. I have seen some companies where it looked like everyone was in their own proverbial boat, doing their own thing, thinking about separate ideas – all moving in different directions. If a crew team were not all rowing in a specific cadence, the boat would get off course; worst-case scenario, it could go backwards or spin in circles! You definitely do not want to be on that team.

The signal caller's job is to look ahead and guide the team in the right direction. I have seen a number of situations where people are working very hard, but they do not have a clear idea of what their plan is. Rowing the wrong way can be as much of an issue with leadership as it can be with the team. In nearly all cases, dysfunctional or unproductive situations stem from poor leadership.

Unlike crew, sports like basketball and football require players to cover different positions. People on a team may play different roles, but they all still have the same goal: to win. If you are just going for the best statistics, but do not care about winning, you may be a superstar – but on a losing team. If everyone is doing their jobs and making sure they are covering for everyone else, then you have a much better chance of winning.

This goes for individuals, teams and companies. Without a clearly set direction and process for measuring your progress along the way, you are apt to make a lot of mistakes – and waste a lot of time and money. Worst of all, you can lose, or fail as a business. A team is simply a group of people formed together to compete with the goal of winning a competition. This is the case in sport or in business.

A lot of times, entrepreneurs decide to start their own businesses because they do not want to work for anyone else. That is not necessarily a bad reason to become an entrepreneur – as long as you are going to be a solopreneur. However, if you are going to be working with and for others, you need to be a team player. Even a CEO needs to rely heavily on their team – and if they are good, they are instrumental in setting the direction of the company.

Work ethic is another critical quality for team members. If you have immense talent, but a poor work ethic, you will never be a champion. This is evident in both sports and in business – areas that require talent and hard work. Startups require commitment to a vision and passion. The work is too hard and too disappointing if you do not believe. Yet, working hard does not mean that you cannot have fun. The times I have worked the hardest have been some of the most fun – because my team was winning and accomplishing great things. In business, you play the game to win – not just to play.

The best teams, in both sports and business, have a collaborative approach. Teammates talk to each other, and the coach talks to the team. The leader sets the direction, but relies on the team to execute. Even though you collaborate with other people, it's still very important to remember that everyone you hire has a clearly defined role that they are responsible for executing on.

Some people advocate keeping roles "loose and flexible." In my experience, that does not work very well – in sports teams or companies. It does not mean that you do not give people autonomy to exercise outside their role, but they have to get their primary role done first. Think about it this way – a wide receiver on a football team should not try to play the role of an offensive tackle, guard or a running back. They have a specific task that they have to accomplish. It does not mean that if someone misses his block, you do not have to cover that block. Once people understand their role, their ability to collaborate and get things done is greatly enhanced.

When you are building a company, you need to decide early what kind of culture you want to have – then hire both for talent and for fit. You want to hire the best and brightest people who have a good style and cultural match with your company. Try to find people who are smarter than you. It is to be hoped that they are a lot smarter than you in their area of specialization. Then "set the bar" high. It's what they call big, hairy, audacious goals. If you expect mediocrity, you are probably going to get mediocrity. If you expect greatness, at least you have a chance at greatness. If you have an attitude that you are going to win, the chances are greatly enhanced that you will win. If you go into a competition with a defeatist attitude, you significantly decrease your chances of winning. Attitude is a huge part of leadership.

It's setting your standards high, having the right goals, holding people accountable and making sure the job is done. This does not mean pestering people or micromanaging them. If you have capable people, you can focus on the **what**, and not the **how**. In other words, focus on the results – what needs to be done – and let the employee focus on how to get it done. As a leader, especially of a fragile startup, you must stay abreast of progress and intervene or apply pressure, as appropriate, when things are not on track.

Talent acquisition can be a tricky process. The first thing you have to do is define roles and responsibilities, then identify the right skills and abilities to fit those roles. You should scout for talent. Look for talent at industry trade shows and universities. Network in order to find the brightest and best people you can. Then turn on the charm. Sell the candidate on your idea. That's another good barometer: if you have a good idea, the best and brightest people are going to be naturally attracted to your idea and your passion around it. You can clearly articulate how things are going to go.

Then you have to recruit these people – get them on board, and help make them as productive as possible as quickly as practical. Remember the boat analogy that I used before? Jim Collins, the author of the best-selling business books *Built to Last* and *Good to Great,* uses the analogy of a bus instead of a boat: "Great companies get the right people on the bus, the wrong people off the bus and the right people in the right seats." When it comes to the boat, you need to have the right people on board, the wrong people off – and make sure that they are all rowing in the same direction.

Make sure everyone in the company knows the common mission and objectives so that they feel they are winning as the company is winning.

A huge part of leadership is setting a vision and understanding the end result so that people can see it, feel it and taste it. It's about outlining a mission to get there, and telling your employees what you are going to do, from a strategic plan standpoint. You need to set clearly defined goals and milestones. Make sure everyone in the company knows the common mission and objectives so that they feel they are winning as the company is winning. This is a big problem in a lot of companies. The employees feel detached from what is going on, since they are doing such a small part of the overall mission. They wonder how their tasks tie into and contribute to the total picture. This is why I like the approach of "management by walking around" – talking with the team, getting to know them, listening to their issues, and explaining to them how what they are doing contributes to the big picture. The more they believe in and have a passion for what they are doing, the more likely they will buy into your idea – and display the willingness to do whatever it takes to win.

As General and President Eisenhower said, "Leadership is the art of getting someone else to do something you want done **because they want to do it**." You have to fuel the passion inside the people on your team. A lot of managers undertake the hiring process simply by looking at roles, skills, responsibilities and abilities. These things are important – but they are not all there is. Are your team members going to be excited about what they are doing? How can you get them there?

Another part of leadership involves game time coaching. A significant part of what great coaches do is **game planning**, and **game management**. They teach and train the team members what to do and make sure they are prepared for certain situations. Two great examples of this are Duke's Mike Krzyzewski, the winningest coach in college basketball, and the New England Patriot's head coach, Bill Belichick, who has won five Super Bowl championships, has taken his teams deep in the playoffs every year, and is the second winningest NFL coach behind Vince Lombardi.

All the great football coaches and quarterbacks always talk about watching a lot of film and studying the competition. Then when it's game time, they know how to react. Of course, the circumstances of the game sometimes dictate a different set of plays. For instance – if you are down by three touchdowns and you only have a quarter left to play, you better ramp-up your passing game! It's the same in business. Sometimes you can execute your exact business plan, while other times you need to adjust, in which case you need an agile team that can adjust, like my team on the DirecTV project.

Sports teams have an advantage in that they must prepare game by game. Companies can emulate this by establishing clear goals that can be measured and ensuring not only that the entire team understands the goals and their roles, but that the whole team celebrates success and key accomplishments.

There is a lot of uncertainty and ambiguity in fast-moving businesses and industries – especially in startups. A lot of things can happen that will force you to adjust and adapt your initial plan to the real-time circumstances taking place around you. There are innumerable examples of this in the startup world, and it is natural that this is the case. Startups are doing something new and innovative. They are not just duplicating what is already in place. As customers use the new product or service, they provide feedback. This causes you to adjust and make refinements. Good coaches, strong leaders, and excellent startup CEOs know how to observe, adjust, lead their teams, and respond to the comments from customers. Great leaders align people in a positive direction and have them moving towards a common goal, then make sure that everyone on the team enjoys the victory.

Perhaps one of most important qualities for a CEO or leader is to **know him or herself**. Know what your **strengths and weaknesses** are, and be able to distinguish between them. Focus on your strengths and hire for your weaknesses. Identify your skills and abilities, as well as your management style.

I like to say **my management style is situational** – it is different depending upon the situation at hand. To use an analogy, you would operate differently if your house were burning to the ground versus a time when you were building a new house. In times of great urgency and importance, you get very short sighted and address key issues at hand. You involve yourself more directly, and become more directional in your leadership style. If the house is burning down, you make sure that everyone either grabs a bucket of water or a fire hose to put the fire out! When you are executing on long-term strategies, you can be more goal oriented versus task oriented. In other words, when you are building houses, you can delegate and coach. You can assess results and give critical feedback. The focus can be on monitoring outcomes.

Situational leadership also depends on the experience and expectations of individuals that you are managing. When dealing with two people with a different level of experience, you wouldn't treat a first line employee or a new college grad the same way you would treat a VP of marketing. You need to have a different set of expectations for people with different levels of responsibility and experience. You would not feed steak to a baby, would you?

Figure out how you want to coach and lead your people. Make sure that the individuals you get on board can work within your style and within your corporate culture – but also that you can adapt your style to different situations and different people. It may be that you have some "difficult personalities" in your organization. You need to critically assess the importance of their contribution versus the challenges of managing these types of people. If a person is critical to meeting the objectives of your organization, then you may need to learn to work with them. It is your job as leader and CEO to adapt your style as much as you can to address the people you have on your team, while at the same time building a cohesive culture for the organization. This is not easy, but it is essential for startup success.

Having an adaptive style can be critically important when you are an outside CEO dealing with company founders. In some ways, starting a company is like starting a revolution. If you want to start a revolution, you need to have anarchists. An anarchist typically despises authority. Clearly there will be tension and friction in a situation like this. Sometimes it means that you, as the CEO, need to eat a lot of humble pie. It is a delicate balancing act. It can also mean deciding when someone is creating more collateral damage than positive results, and taking action at that time. Your judgment will determine whether they are worth keeping on board, or are more of a liability than an asset. These are the real-life and very tough situations that you must deal with as a startup CEO and a leader.

Mentors, Advisers and Your Board of Directors as an Extension of Your Team

Excellent entrepreneurs cultivate and heed the advice of mentors. Strong mentors and advisers are an extension of your team that you can leverage with customers, suppliers, partners, and potential investors. Especially as a new entrepreneur or first time CEO, you can leverage the experience of your advisers as a way to boost the credibility of your company.

Great entrepreneurs foster relationships with more seasoned and experienced people. This allows them to learn things at an accelerated rate, which would not be possible if they tried to learn everything on their own, or if they only assessed situations based solely on their personal perspective and "lens" versus looking at things from the vantage point of experienced and trusted advisers as well. Like great athletes, great entrepreneurs want the best coaches, and the best guidance. This is how you become great. This is all about a great entrepreneur's willingness to learn, and not just from books, but also from other seasoned and experienced people.

There are three major types of relationships and constituencies you need to build in your extended team as the leader of a startup:

1. Mentors and Coaches
2. Advisory Boards
3. The Board of Directors

Mentors and Coaches

Having a mentor or coach can be one of the most beneficial things you can do as a startup CEO. The key is to find a person with the "right stuff," which includes:

- Domain expertise in your field or market focus
- Technical expertise in your product area
- Good coaching skills
- Good personality fit with you

In an earlier chapter we talked about Eric Schmidt, then CEO of Google, enlisting the help of Bill Campbell, the former CEO and Chairman of Intuit, as a mentor and coach. Mr. Schmidt was not the only Silicon Valley executive that used Mr. Campbell as a mentor, but the combination of the match in skill set and personality was key for the relationship to be successful.

Bill Campbell is what I would call a "head coach" type of mentor. He had experience in a similar job, and could relay that experience to his mentee. As a seasoned executive, you gain a sense of what works and what doesn't work in different situations. You develop an intuition about things that typically does not exist without experience, regardless of how smart you are. I think this type of mentorship is critical, if not essential, to being a successful startup CEO.

A second type of coaching is what is called "strength coaching." These are executive coaches who look at things from a personal dynamic and human resources standpoint. They typically conduct "360-degree feedback," or comments from your boss, your direct reports, and your peers. They use instruments to assess your strengths, weaknesses, personality type, intellect, and biases. These coaches then use this information to help you become a better manager and a better leader. This type of coaching can also be very valuable, but it is not a replacement for a solid head coach type of mentor.

Advisory Boards

Depending on your company, your target market, and your level of experience, it can be very valuable to build both business and technical advisory boards for your company. Business advisers frequently have domain expertise in your target markets, and technical advisers typically have specialized knowledge in either your product area or the product area of your target customers.

A **business advisory board** is typically composed of customers, customers' customers, retired customers, and partners that have extensive experience in dealing with your target customer base. They can provide insight to help you navigate through the business process of getting your product adopted by your target customers.

Similarly, a technical advisory board is frequently composed of technical experts at your target customers, retired customers, academics, and experts in some specific area of regulation or international adoption. They have extensive experience in dealing with the PESTEL – Political, Economic, Social, Technological, Environmental, and Legal analysis – and technical issues of your target customer base. They can provide insight to help you navigate through the technical process of getting your product adopted by your target customers.

I am a proponent of advisory boards when you are dealing with any complex B2B or B2C sales process. Enlisting the insight and support of industry insiders can be very beneficial to your chances of success.

Boards of Directors

One of the most challenging aspects of being a CEO is working for and managing a board of directors. If you have had a successful career and worked your way up through organizations, you have a familiarity with having a single boss, or in some matrix organizations, maybe two bosses. However, once you become a CEO you are both the overall "boss" of the company, and you have five to seven bosses on the startup board of directors. You are also expected to lead board meetings. It is much different and presents a different set of challenges.

The startup board of a company is there to manage the CEO, focus on strategy and risk and reward, and to represent the company shareholders. Considering my experience of being a serial entrepreneur, running three companies, and serving on multiple for-profit and non-profit boards, I have included some of my thoughts on the topic of managing your board.

If you are a company founder, then you are fortunate to be able to build your board of directors with people that you feel can help you to achieve the goals and your vision for the company. However, as soon as you make the decision to raise outside money, there may be a requirement to add an investor, or multiple investors, to your board of directors. These board members are usually Angel investors or venture capitalists. Sometimes the board member can be an executive from a strategic partner that has made an investment in your company. Under all these situations, it is important that you understand who will get a board seat in your company when you raise this capital, and work hard to find investors who will be board members supportive of your company vision.

In addition to the company founders and outside investors, there are usually one or two industry experts that you want to have on your board of directors. These "outside directors" can be important advisers and sounding boards, both to you and to the investor board members in the company. If the CEO of the company is not a founder, then he or she will usually be on the board of directors as well. I would never recommend becoming the CEO of a company unless you are on the board of directors.

In selecting board members, you need to make sure that these are people that you trust. They know how to treat confidential information, and they do not have conflicts of interest other than the inherent conflict with being a strategic partner or an investor in the company. Ideally, you want board members who are smart, experienced, thoughtful, calm, empathetic, and who possess significant domain expertise or technical expertise in your vertical markets and technologies.

Ideally, you want a board that works as a team for the betterment of the company – they are all committed to the success of the company. Great board members bring a set of unique and complementary experiences, perspectives and skills to the boardroom. It is very valuable to have board members with significant CEO experience, ideally spanning multiple companies, and both public and private companies. It is also very valuable to have board members with experience in raising capital. Many board members have "Type A" personalities and many are so-called Alpha Males. However, I think it is invaluable to have diversity on the board, as long as you do not sacrifice expertise in the process.

In a couple of my companies, I had "board observers" in addition to board members. Board observers are usually strategic partners, and they can frequently have conflicts of interest, and even be competitive with each other. It is important to manage and navigate through these conflicts and ensure that confidential information of the company, its customers, partners, and supplier remains confidential.

In both private and public companies, it is important to have the right level of involvement of the management team, apart from the CEO. I am a proponent of giving key executives exposure to the board, but this needs to be managed properly. If your management team is involved in board meetings, then it is important to have an executive session that is only attended by the CEO and other board members. This is a requirement in public companies, but I think it is a good practice for private companies as well.

As mentioned above, I am a proponent of diversity on the board. This includes women, people of color, academics, various technical experts, business functional experts, and market ecosystem experts. Getting different perspectives has immense value. The importance is to maintain a strong team dynamic and collaborative spirit. It is also very important to have people with CEO experience, ideally with experience in your vertical markets. I am also a proponent of building business and technical advisory boards. This is a way to solicit expertise without the burden of fiduciary responsibility.

I cannot emphasize enough the importance of having domain expertise in your vertical markets on the board. It is important when the business is doing well because you can leverage their network and experience in how to grow the company, and how to risk-assess opportunities and various strategies. However, board members with CEO experience and domain expertise can be just as important, and maybe even more valuable, during times of adversity for the company. These board members can be a sounding board apart from the company CEO, and can provide perspective based on their own experience.

In assembling a board of directors, it is important to have people who have sufficient expertise and experience running the key committees: Compensation, Audit, and Nominating & Corporate Governance. This means that you need at least one person with a strong accounting background. This is critical in a public company, but still very important in private companies. If a company is involved in M&A discussions, it can also be helpful to establish an ad hoc strategy committee. This can help significantly in keeping a process moving forward without the need to assemble the full board for every little discussion. Some board members may resist this, but I have found this to be a valuable tool.

The CEO is expected to lead the board meeting. I have never seen a case where this is not true in companies that I have run and in companies and non-profits where I have been a board member. It is one of the most challenging roles for a CEO to simultaneously be the leader of the company while having all the other board members as your bosses.

I have been in situations where I have held both the CEO and the Chairman of the Board titles, and situations where I have only held the CEO title. Both can work, but I prefer to have an outside independent board member as Chairman. Sometimes a founder may have the Chairman title and still have an executive position in the company. I have found that this is typically a ceremonial title and not really of much value to the CEO, the company or the board. If the CEO and the Chairman have a good working relationship, the Chairman can be the "broker" of the board meeting agenda topics and help with the flow of board meetings when it is awkward or difficult for the CEO to provide an extra push on certain board members.

Typically, in private companies that are not profitable, board members are compensated with equity. In profitable public companies, the compensation is more commonly a combination of equity and cash. Good board members are usually comfortable with equity, and this provides the best alignment of interest with shareholders.

The Compensation Committee for the board also sets compensation for the CEO and has a say in other executive compensation. The full board is involved in approving of the business plan and financial model, as well as the equity compensation plan and structure. As such, the board has a big influence on compensation of all the employees. It is critically important that you, as the CEO, are able to persuade the board to support a compensation structure that will allow you to attract and retain key talent for the company. I have found that using third party benchmarking is very effective, and it is a requirement for public companies. I have also found that equity compensation is the key carrot for most employees, especially executives, but it is difficult to get most people to work without reasonably competitive wages and benefits, unless they are very young and single and willing to take more equity, or they have already had a large exit.

The other critical part of compensation for executives is what happens in a **change of control - when the company is sold - or** what happens when a key executive or company founder is **terminated without cause**. The company needs to have **employment agreements** for the founders and key executives, so it is clear how these key employee situations are to be handled, if one of these circumstances happens. Doing this is essential to attracting and retaining top talent in the organization.

The CEO Needs to "Manage" the Board of Directors

Boards want to see seemingly contradictory characteristics in their CEOs, and this requires you to strike a delicate balance. They want you to be a leader, but also someone who can take direction. They want someone who is confident, but not cocky. They want to see someone who is passionate and who has conviction but is also receptive to their ideas and remains calm.

I think it is critical for a CEO to be confident and passionate. However, his or her confidence needs to be grounded in experience, facts, and conviction to their cause. At the same time, a board wants a CEO who is receptive to their suggestions and guidance. Boards want someone who will take constructive comments with grace and style. I have been in innumerable board situations where I was fighting for something that I believed in. Some board members would say, "Patrick is stubborn. Patrick isn't listening. Patrick is defensive." Fortunately for me, in many of these circumstances, other board members would say, "He is listening, but he just does not agree with you. And neither do I." It is a delicate balance, and you will need to learn what works best for you to accomplish the key things that you need for your company, and take critical feedback in stride.

If someone ever says, "We do not have any politics in our company or on our board," they are simply naïve, lying or incompetent. An effective CEO needs to be humble and have a balance between listening and leading.

I have found one of the most effective ways to do this is to pre-sell ideas before the board meeting. I always make an effort to reach out to each of the board members, and cover the key points I plan to cover in the board meeting so they understand where I am looking for support. Understanding the power structure of the board is also critically important to get support from the board on your key agenda items.

Public companies are required to follow federally mandated guidelines for risk management, and many large companies have established Enterprise Risk Management (ERM) processes. Although this level of structure and process is not necessarily required or desired in a startup, it is important to have some form of **risk assessment** on every key strategic decision. The CEO should outline the risks to board members.

Whenever you are in a time of business crisis, you need to shorten focus and milestones, while maintaining a longer-term perspective on the big picture. What do I mean by this? In a time of crisis, some board members may panic. It is primarily a response to their personal reputation possibly being damaged. The CEO as the leader needs to stay "calm in the storm," and instill confidence that all issues that can be addresses are being addressed. The board also may have a tendency to blame outside factors on the CEO. This is where all the hard work you have put in to build credibility and trust with the board comes into play. It is also where having an outside board member with deep domain expertise and experience can be helpful. In times like these, I try to provide lots of transparency to the board, and over-communicate. I give more detailed information to the board and I give more frequent updates. I work to show progress by discussing specific near-term milestones and progress.

Board meetings should really focus on the bigger strategic issues, but board members, especially in startups, want an update on customer traction and progress. These tactical updates should be handled in a consistent format at the beginning of the meeting. I like tracking milestones and giving updates in an executive dashboard format. I also always give an update on financials and burn rate in a startup that is not profitable. I have found that it is best to compare progress versus plan. I like to explain the annual operating plan with monthly granularity. In startup situations, you may need to make quarterly adjustments to annual plans depending upon progress and financial runway. I have found that different board members have different sets of expectations about how much information should be delivered in board meetings. It is important that you strike a balance amongst the various board members and take into account the power structure within the board. If possible, work to get some type of alignment of expectations. It will make your life easier, and it will make board meetings more effective. If there are certain board members who want more information, you can always give it to them outside of the board meeting.

The other critical thing is to bring solutions when you raise problems with the board. Just dumping your problems on the board is not showing leadership. If you want to brainstorm about solutions, do it with your team, your mentor, or a board member close with you outside the board meeting. Socialize the most significant problems and your proposed solutions to individual board members before the board meeting.

As a wise man once said, "Success has many fathers, but failure is an orphan." In the case of a startup, it is important that the CEO accepts responsibly for "failures" and that he or she shares the success with their team and the board. You need to be very careful what you say about individuals on your team in front of the board. Board members, and especially VCs, may make snap judgments about what should be done, and you want to ensure that you do not cause disruption when there is not really a need for it. Set goals that are achievable. Set revenue targets and expense budgets that are achievable. Build momentum by meeting key milestones. Celebrate success with the team, but do not rest on your laurels. Share the wins and use them as a way to build momentum.

Decisions and adjustments like these speak to the overall culture of your organization, which we will look at in more detail in the next chapter.

CHAPTER 10

Creating a Culture of Getting Things Done

In the *PLAN COMMIT WIN Methodology*, building a successful team is all about innovation and execution, yet many organizations frequently overlook the importance of execution – and startups are no exception. It is essential to finish things on time and on budget, while meeting all the customer's key requirements. Remember the basic tenets of this approach: **plan the course, set milestones, and measure results.** You need to develop and encourage a culture that helps you get these things done.

We have already discussed how one of a startup's greatest competitive advantages is speed – in decision-making, and in execution. However, even when you do not make a decision, you need to embrace the fact that you are effectively making a decision by not making a decision.

Figure 10.1 - Hierarchy for Raising Capital - Execute

In the context of funding your business, you need to execute on plans that deliver step function improvements in valuation – things that validate your business model and reduce risk. This section will dig into the details about the milestones that move the needle for investors. It is important to understand what motivates venture capitalists and Angel investors. Company founders and CEOs frequently assume that investors should put money into their companies because they are taking big risks – and therefore potentially offer huge rewards. However, the VC wants to find a deal with a mismatch of risk and valuation. They believe that they have a better ability to assess risk-reward, and thus can have an arbitrage situation. They are willing to give up some liquidity as a result, if the potential returns are great enough.

Setting Key Milestones and a Bias Toward Action

Your annual operating plan, AOP, your annual financial budget, and your annual headcount budget contain all the key milestones that you need to manage and run your business. However, in business and in life you are sometimes faced with unforeseen and unfortunate events. Under these circumstances, you will need to revise the milestones that you established in your annual plan. There are many reasons why this could happen – some inside your control and others outside your control. Maybe you have made a course correction based on customer feedback, and maybe you have even made a major pivot. The key here is that the plan is the plan, until you make a conscious decision to change the **plan of record**, or the plan that is currently in place. Successful companies have a plan and they adjust their plan, as required, but they are not **constantly** changing the plan.

My solution for this problem is quarterly goals that are based on the annual plan. If we have made a big change in course, for the right reasons, then we adjust and restate or change key milestones, and have a new plan of record. Keep in mind that course corrections and adjustments are not a change in the overall mission. If you board an airplane from New York-JFK to London-Heathrow and you hit bad weather, you still want to get to London safely, and ideally close to on time. Course corrections like changing the priority of customers or priorities of product features due to customer feedback are like that. You adjust the tactics, but the strategy remains the same, and the big vision and big goals remain the same. It is only in the case of a significant pivot that you change your overall strategy. That is why companies that have more than one or two pivots at most usually fail.

They say that the smartest people make more bad decisions than anyone else, because they make more decisions than anyone else. What is important is to have a high percentage of right decisions. The other key is to make decisions and adjust to keep things moving forward. You need to have that **bias towards action** but also the ability to keep your eyes open and **course-correct along the way**.

You must also maintain a heartfelt belief that you can win and keep your team on board with that – and be able make the level of self-sacrifice necessary for startups. Some people get this and some people do not. Some people dislike the uncertainty and ambiguity associated with startups, and are therefore more suited to work in a bigger, more corporate environment. However, in my experience, the startup experience becomes very gratifying once you have achieved some major accomplishments.

I am from Missouri, born and raised in St. Louis, so I know that Missouri is "The Show Me State" – as in, if I had a dollar for every time a customer said to me, "I'm from Missouri: you have to show me," I would be a very wealthy man! When you are a startup looking to raise outside capital, you should treat all Angel investors and venture capitalists as though they were from Missouri. They want to see a track record of execution and that you have achieved key milestones.

Not that much has been written about execution – quite frankly, because it's boring compared to strategy, product positioning, and marketing. However, execution is an important concept for all CEOs to grasp. Larry Bossidy from AlliedSignal said in his book *Execution: The Discipline of Getting Things Done*, "Many people regard execution as detailed work that's beneath their dignity. That's wrong. To the contrary, it's the leader's most important job." I believe that wholeheartedly. You need to lead by example. You need to work hard, and set goals. Measure people against those goals, and hold them accountable. Without that, you are not going to accomplish very much as a startup. The most meaningful areas of execution in a startup or growth company are the achievement of key milestones that mitigate risk. As risk decreases, valuation increases.

Measuring Results

How do you know if you are executing your plan successfully? You need to measure results – particularly the ones that are most important to prospective investors: those that reduce risk and increase value. Key factors for reducing risk – especially in a startup or growth company – include:

Status of Product Development

- Pre-product
- Demonstration
- Prototype
- Alpha phase – you can demonstrate your product in the lab, but it isn't ready to sample to customers
- Beta phase – you are sampling it to customers but it's not suitable for going into production

- Minimum Viable Product (MVP) – suitable for sales into some segments, and great for getting validated learning from customers
- Product in production

Status of Your Revenue

- Pre-revenue
- Development revenue: development money from consulting, non-recurring engineering, or some type of research revenue from strategic partners
- Grants: development funding from the government
- Revenue for your initial product from a single customer
- Revenue from multiple customers (customer diversification)
- Revenue from multiple customers in different market segments (market diversification)
- Revenue from additional products (product diversification)

As a company makes progress in establishing its business model, it reduces risk, and thus increases valuation. Here are some key risks that investors consider either explicitly or implicitly:

- **Product Risk**: Does your product work in the target customer's application how you promised and how they want it to work?
- **Market Risk**: Validating the size and growth of your target market by winning a critical mass of customers purchasing products, and giving more information to validate CAC and LTV.
- **Product-Market Risk**: Validating your business model including revenue, gross margins and operating margins at levels where you can reasonably extrapolate a financial picture that validates your business model assumptions.
- **Competitive Risk**: Beating competition, substitute products, and new entrants validates the strength of your competitive position in the market.
- **Operational Risk**: You can scale product deployment manufacturing with high quality and reliability. There are few customer complaints, and none that disrupt product sales.

- **Legal Risk**: Are you being attacked through litigation? How is the risk assessment on this?
- **Intellectual Property Protection Risk**: You have done a good job protecting your IP with patents, trade secrets, copyrights, and trademarks. Have you adequately used Non-Disclosure Agreements?
- **Employment Risk**: Do you have excellent human resource policies, government compliance, training, employment contracts, non-disclosure agreements, proprietary invention agreements, and executive employment agreements?
- **Team Risk**: Do you have a strong team with key core competencies and advisers with credibility, functional, technical, market and domain expertise?

All of these things show that your company has less risk, especially if your target customers are potentially large and growing fast. Valuation increases in step functions – and each of these risk reductions increases valuation.

Smart investors will track your progress towards your key milestones. Meeting milestones also establishes a track record and builds trust. Establishing credibility is essential with investors – even if you have to borrow it from your advisers in the beginning.

You cannot successfully scale a business without a stellar team and world-class execution. Timing is also very important; however, you'll be able to tell a lot about the suitability of your timing if you've run a thorough strategic planning process.

The Fish That Almost Got Away: Entropic's Pivot

Back in 2004, when Entropic was still a private company, we were having difficulty getting traction with our highest value end customers for adoption of our MoCA (Multimedia over Coax Alliance) home networking solution. You'll recall from earlier in the book that MoCA enabled room-to-room streaming of video, which is the underlying technology for multi-room DVR. The major cable and satellite TV operators were more focused on single-room DVR, and the move to HDTV service. These cable TV and satellite TV operators also controlled the Pay TV market in the US at the time; cable had about 70 percent market share and satellite had 30 percent.

Then, seemingly out of the blue, Verizon and AT&T both decided to enter the Pay TV business – and suddenly, we had two new potential customers. One of our founders –the Vice President of business development – decided, after some coaxing from me and the other founders, to pursue this business. We secured a design commitment with both Verizon and AT&T.

After six months, we had lost AT&T for a number of reasons – and we were dangerously close to losing Verizon. The MoCA Alliance included Comcast, Time Warner Cable, and EchoStar/Dish Network, but Verizon was not a member. There was some reluctance inside Entropic for getting a telco involved in the alliance – and some reluctance with the existing MoCA members toward letting Verizon have an inside seat. After a lot of heated internal meetings, the founding team and I agreed on working to get Verizon onto the MoCA board of directors. My team had to do a lot of "selling" to the other alliance members – but we got it done. Entropic went public in 2007 based primarily on the strength of the ramp in the MoCA business in the Verizon-FiOS deployment. Due to the Great Recession, the next major Pay TV launch of MoCA did not happen until 2010.

All startups will face a number of these turning points – moments when you need to make tough decisions in an uncertain environment. I have heard that the winner at the World Series of Poker has to go All-In at least six times to have a chance to get to the final table. Knowledge, experience, and gut-feel all have a role in these decisions. However, you can always make things better if there is passionate and committed involvement from the team. The right answers always look obvious in hindsight; but of course, they are rarely obvious when you are making them.

Without strong mentorship, leadership, open discussion, a bias toward action, and a solid decision-making process, the probability of making the right decisions diminishes. Outside investors will not bet on your company unless they see a strong team and a solid track record. Even if you have a spectacular idea, if the investor feels that your team cannot pull it off, then they will not invest. In the next chapter, we take a closer look at the investor pitch and presentation.

CHAPTER 11

Attracting the Right Investors

And now, for the part of the book you have been anticipating: getting your company funded! It might seem like there was a lot of lead-up to this "main event" – but you want to make absolutely sure that you have everything in place before you begin courting investors. Why? Because you will waste your precious and valuable time. As the CEO you do need to spend time ensuring that you have sufficient capital to grow your business, but you also need to focus on product development, winning customers, driving revenue, and building a company track record. It is likely that efforts to raise money from professional investors without adequate preparation will be fruitless, so it could be a major waste of time and a huge opportunity cost.

Figure 11.1 - Hierarchy for Raising Capital - Pitch

Once you have developed a solid business plan, you will want to:

1. Create the right investor marketing materials
2. Build your investment team
3. Cultivate your network
4. Develop an investor funnel; and
5. Begin to cultivate investors.

Running a startup company involves constant selling, and not only to customers. You are selling to your board, your employees, partners, management team, family, friends, and professional network – and, of course, prospective investors in the company. In the context of the *PLAN COMMIT WIN Methodology*, this requires that you articulate results and outline the plan for taking the company to the next level. These principles are really designed for companies that have made significant progress on their business during the bootstrapping and friends and family stages of financing for their company.

You should plan for the process of raising outside capital to take three to six months. Do not forget that one of the biggest selling points of your business is you and your team. Now that you have a plan, commitment, and a track record, you will have to undertake the following steps to secure investors. Here is a roadmap of key steps in the process of raising outside capital for your company:

Building a Target List of Investors

1. Identify Key Investors with Domain Expertise in Your Vertical Market
2. Create a Target Investor List
3. Farm Your Network for Introductions to Key Investors
4. Identify the Ideal Investors for Your Company
5. Approach Domain Experts in Your Space to Get Feedback & Endorsements

Creating and Perfecting the Presentation and Funding Materials

6. Create an Executive Summary
7. Create an Investor Presentation
8. Create an "Elevator Pitch"
9. Develop Frequently Asked Questions (FAQ)
10. Test Your Executive Summary and Investor Presentation with "Friendly" Domain Experts for Feedback and Refinement
11. Practice Your Investor Presentation Using a Video Camera
12. Practice Your Investor Presentation with a Simulated Hostile Audience and "Devil's Advocate"
13. Refine Exec Summary, Investor Pitch, and FAQs
14. Prepare materials for Due Diligence

Meeting Preparation and Follow-Up

15. Learn as much as you can about your target investor as possible before your meeting with him or her

16. Set a Goal for Each Investor Meeting
17. Use Your Network for Warm Introductions to Key Investors, but NOT Initially on Your Top Investor Prospect
18. Refine Investor Marketing Materials After Each Meeting
19. Follow-up on Any Investor Questions That You Did Not Answer in the Meeting
20. Once You Feel Very Solid, Approach the Top Investor Prospects and Use Warm Introductions
21. Keep Prospective Investors Abreast of Your Progress Versus Key Milestones

Choosing and Closing Your Investor Group
22. Focus Your Investor Selection on the Current Round and the Long Term Process of Building Your Company
23. Hire a Competent Attorney to Help with All Legal Documents
24. Set-Up a Data Room for Due Diligence Materials
25. Understand Key Terms for Negotiation of a Term Sheet

Identification of Target Investors

The first step is to create a list of target investors, focusing on individuals with domain expertise in your target markets, or technical expertise in your product area. Target investors should include corporate strategic investors, as well as Angel investors or venture capital firms. Angel investors will typically be involved in Seed rounds, and some Series A financings. VCs will be involved is some Series A financings, and more typically in growth stage financings: Series B and C. These days it is much less likely that VCs will invest in a Seed financing round.

Use resources like Crunchbase, Angel.co, Mattermark, CB Insights, and VB Profiles to create your target list. Look for investors who make investments in your industry sector, and at your stage of investment. It is perfectly fine to meet Angel investor groups as well. Even if you are not in front of the "right" investors each time you present your story, professional investors look to each other for deal ideas. You should put investors who have had successful exits in your industry sector on your list as well, if you can find them. You should also look for technical experts in academia as a source for investment and leads.

Working an Investor "Sales Process"

A warm introduction to investors is key with most Angel investors and nearly all VCs. One way to connect with an investor on your target list is to look at resources like LinkedIn and Angel.co to see if you know someone who can introduce you to that person. Work your network! If you do not have a well-established network, reach out to people who have technical or domain expertise and cultivate them as mentors and advisers. Do not approach them for investment, though; if they are interested enough, they will ask to invest.

If you can secure an introduction, the next step is to write a friendly email in which you send your executive summary. Include:

- Your name and contact information
- A little bit about yourself, your team, and your company
- Give a mini-elevator pitch in writing

The objective of the email is to get a meeting. If you got a warm introduction, then thank the person who made the introduction in the email and move them to BCC. If your email captures their interest, they may want to have a call or even an in-person meeting. When you have the call, give them your best elevator pitch and be ready to answer questions. You may even want to share a few slides. The purpose of both the executive summary and the telephone elevator pitch is to get a face-to-face meeting.

When meeting with investors, **be prepared**. Prepare your homework on the investor. Look at their background. What investments have they have made in the past? What is their technical and domain expertise? Are they a generalist or a specialist? Do they lead financing rounds? Do they co-lead? Whom do they co-invest with? What is their track record? Are they the lead partner and decision maker at the firm? Be ready to engage in a dialogue and to answer questions. Have a clear objective for the meeting and a clear call to action at the end. If you get a question that you cannot answer, cover what you can and commit to following up, then do that promptly after the meeting. And do not worry: if you have followed the process outlined in this book, you will be more prepared than 90 to 95 percent of all entrepreneurs.

Figure 11.2 - Investor Funnel

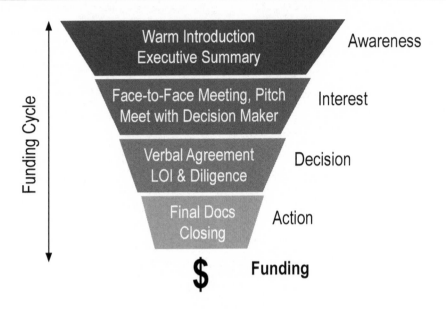

Key Materials – Tools in Your Toolbox

You know by now that the **executive summary** from your business plan can serve as a standalone marketing document. The next thing you need to prepare is your **investor presentation**. This presentation should provide enough information to investors that they will ask for a second meeting. You want to have an "**elevator pitch**" – an overview of what your company does, your customers, the problem you solve, your solution, your unique value proposition, and your competitive advantage. You should be able to deliver this in one or two minutes.

Prepare a **deeper dive presentation**, which is really a PowerPoint version of your **business plan**, as well as a Word version for people who prefer to read a document instead. You also need to have a **financial plan**.

Another thing that you need to prepare, that you likely will not share directly with investors, is a set of Frequently Asked Questions, or **FAQs**, and your answers. Use your team playing Devil's advocates and your key friendly advisers to prepare the FAQs. Once you have a good set of answers, go through live Q&A with your team. Make sure the answers make sense and clearly deal with the questions. The FAQ is not a static document. As you meet with investors, you will continue to add to it. It is much better to have this document than just carrying these answers in your head. You need to answer things consistently, and you need to have key members of your team aligned with you.

The Importance of Getting Attention and Telling a Story

If you manage to gain a face-to-face meeting with investors, you need to capture their interest in the first five minutes. This is short attention span theatre. VCs see hundreds of deals, and only invest in a handful – so you have to tell a compelling story. You must convey the customer problem that you are solving, how your solution will solve that problem, and how you will win customers. My good friend Oren Klaff, who wrote the Foreword to this book, is also the author of *Pitch Anything* – a terrific book about the psychology of buyers, and a wonderful resource to help you create your investor pitch and presentation. I also worked with a presentation coach named Jerry Weissman before taking Entropic public. Jerry has a couple good books about presenting as well: *Presenting to Win: The Art of Telling Your Story* and *In the Line of Fire: How to Handle Tough Questions – When It Counts*.

Both of these gentlemen emphasize the importance of using stories in your presentation – which is critical. Even if you can spin an amazing yarn, if you do not have a real idea, a solid plan, a commitment to win, a stellar team, and a track record of execution, you will still struggle to get funded. Securing funding is about psychology, trust, confidence and content.

Content of the Investor Presentation

It should not come as a surprise that you should focus your investor presentation on the business. As discussed earlier in this book, many new entrepreneurs or technical CEOs have a tendency to spend 90 percent of the investor presentation talking about their product. Investors want to maybe use 20 percent of the time on the product, and 80 percent on the business model. So focus on what is most important to your audience.

Investors want to receive information in a standard way. Beyond the opening story, follow the flow of the Business Plan outlined in Chapter 8. The purpose of the initial face-to-face meeting is to gain attention and interest, and get on the investor's radar. You want to be able to keep them abreast of progress, and get a second meeting.

I am a major advocate of "storyboarding" your presentation, and ensuring that it covers all key information, but that it also flows. Using the slide sorter feature of PowerPoint is very helpful for this. You should also have a script for your presentation. Practice with the script, make it your own, then throw the script away and improvise. Present with passion and commitment. There is no substitute for preparation. When presenting, stand on the left-hand side of the screen, not in front of the projector. Video tape yourself on your cell phone so you can see how you will appear to investors. There is no substitute for seeing how you look; it can provide invaluable feedback for improving your presentation.

Structure of the Investor Presentation

The first and most important step in an investor presentation is to tell a meaningful, relevant, and compelling story that will capture your audience's attention in the first five minutes. If you do not get them interested early, you are unlikely to have their full attention throughout the remainder of the presentation. Structurally, I recommend that you try to follow the 10-20-30 Rule popularized by Guy Kawasaki, who said that an investor presentation "should have ten slides, last no more than twenty minutes, and contain no font smaller than thirty-point." This is a guideline and not a hard rule. It is also important to include graphics and visual aids where appropriate. For an hour-long investor presentation, structure your presentation for 25 to 30 minutes maximum. If it takes you two to three minutes per slide, that is about 25 minutes for a 10-slide presentation. An introductory story may take another three to four minutes.

So what about all that other time, you might be wondering?

- Assume that other people will be five minutes late. You should be 10 minutes early.
- Assume five minutes for introductions.
- Assume a presentation time of 25 minutes.
- Question and answers should take 10 to 15 minutes, and if the presentation is going well, it will be an interactive conversation with questions during the presentation.
- Five minutes for taking action items and planning next steps.

That is a total of 55 minutes. Finishing early is generally not a problem – but don't use more time and make the meeting go long. Odds are that your audience cannot and probably does not want to stay late. In the unusual circumstance that the investor wants to spend additional time with you, make sure you have scheduled enough time between meetings to accommodate your key target investors. Otherwise, commit to follow up with another meeting or phone call within a short time.

A couple other things to keep in mind that are good practices for presenting:

- The pitch should have a beginning, middle, and an end.
- Tell your audience what you are going to say, say it, and then summarize it.

It might seem simple, but do the following to make sure that people can read and follow your slides:

- Use bullet points where possible.
- Have no more than 4 to 5 bullet points per slide.
- Have no more than 5 to 6 words per bullet.
- Use no more than three colors.
- Use visual aids where possible, and make sure that the audience can read anything that is written on your slides.
- Use compelling graphics, and explain what you are showing in your charts or graphs. Walk through these step-by-step.
- Limit the use of "build" slides, or slides that appear in stages in a PowerPoint presentation.
- Use font styles and font sizes that people over 50 years old can read.
- Use stories and analogies where possible.
- Do not read your slides verbatim, but instead let your slides be your guide.
- Use transition language from slide to slide, and keep transitions consistent.
- Include some type of legend that allows your audience to track with your slides.

Before you present to an audience, look at your slides from the back of a room. Can you read them?

Finally, you will want to have a specific Call-to-Action, or CTA, at the end of the presentation. What do you want from attendees? Usually, it is another meeting. Maybe you are not meeting with the decision maker, and the next step is to get to him or her. Maybe you want to come back with an update once you have hit some key milestones. How much money are you seeking? Investors will want to know why you need that amount of money, the uses of that cash, if you have any flexibility, and what they can expect to get in return. Be bold and ask for what you want.

The Courting Process of Raising Money

Most investors will want to see you a few times, meet some key people on your team, establish trust, see if you can execute, measure your results, then determine whether you can establish a track record. People want to be courted and pursued by their suitor before they date, and date before they get engaged and eventually married. Investors are no different; they want to put their money into people that they know, like and trust. This takes time. It is a process.

Of course, if you are a sought-after entrepreneur in Silicon Valley with a track record of past success and prior investments from the likes of top venture capital firms like Kleiner-Perkins, Sequoia, and Benchmark, then these rules may not apply. You might get term sheets thrown at you by people begging you to let them into your deal. However, it's also likely that you would not be reading this book if you are that person. If this does happen, please call me and tell me about it! I will be really impressed!

I have never had an easy time raising capital for any of my companies. It has always been a difficult and time-consuming process. But there are things you can do to assist in the courting process:

- Set milestones that you expect to meet or even beat in the three to six months it takes to raise a round.
- Keep potential investors abreast of your progress, and let them know when you meet key milestones. I like to use phone calls and face-to-face meetings to do this. It is more interactive than email or a newsletter. As a public company, it is critical that you are familiar with Regulation Fair Disclosure, also known as Reg FD, but this is not a significant issue with privately held companies.

- Use the milestones you have met as a way to establish credibility and a track record, and keep in mind that the opposite occurs if you constantly miss milestones.
- Try to get key decision makers to meet you in a more social setting after the second meeting. Lunches and dinners are best. At least meet for coffee.

Investors invest in ideas, but they also invest in people. Ultimately, you want to create scarcity in your deal. Like it or not, most investors are followers. Everyone is looking for you to get that initial term sheet. A key in the process of raising outside capital is to find your "anchor tenant," or your lead investor. A part of this is knowing who leads investing rounds. Once you have a lead and a term sheet, the interest in your deal will usually ignite, as long as the lead investor is respected in the investor community. Keep in mind that it is more important to get the right investors at a fair valuation, then the wrong investors at a high valuation.

The Technical Process of Raising Money

The most important technical part of raising money is getting the right corporate attorney and a key financial professional on your team. You ideally want an attorney that has a lot of experience working with both startups and venture capital firms – and who has a great deal of experience in mergers and acquisitions (M&A) transactions and in taking companies public in an initial public offering (IPO).

An online electronic professional data room may be required for due diligence. This is where you'll include all the important contracts, agreements, filed and issued patents, and other critical validation of your business. You should also be prepared for the possibility that investors might want to make some calls to current and potential customers. VCs and most Angel investors will not sign Non-Disclosure Agreements unless they are moving to a due diligence phase, which typically happens after there is a Letter of Intent (LOI) to invest in your company.

Valuation is important when negotiating a term sheet – but other deal terms may be even more important. A good attorney will be able to counsel you on what deal terms are standard and non-standard. Some investors might want so-called side letter agreements, so you need to know how to negotiate these. Side letter agreements are used to address special arrangements with certain investors, or unique issues that are specific to only a particular investor or subset of investors. Side letter agreements are used as a means of interpreting, supplementing and even altering the terms contained in primary agreements and other governing documents. A common side letter agreement for a strategic investor in a private company is to have board of director observation rights. Again, an experienced attorney is very helpful here to help give insight about what is common and what is non-standard. If you are raising outside capital, you need **employment agreements** for the founders and any key executives. Your attorney will make sure everything is written correctly in the **definitive agreement** for the financing round.

Navigating an IPO through the Treacherous Waters of the "Sub-Prime Meltdown"

In addition to raising a lot of private capital for my own companies, I also have experience in taking a company public – and raising money in a secondary offering in the public markets. The pool of potential investors and money is a couple orders of magnitude larger in the public markets versus venture capital. There is also liquidity in the stock. Both of these things change the dynamics of raising money; but at the essence, investors want to make bets on companies where they invest in a discontinuity between risk and reward that isn't apparent to everyone else. And again – they only invest in people that they know, like and trust.

When I was with Entropic in late 2006, the Verizon FiOS deployment prompted a massive ramp in our business. We were so successful that the price that potential acquirers were willing to pay for Entropic was far below what we could get in the public markets, based on our banker's assessment.

However, I felt that we were sub-scale for a public company, and we lacked enough product line and customer diversification. Another private company in San Diego called RF Magic was operating under a similar set of circumstances. While they were a little behind us in revenue, they were ahead of us in gross margin expansion. They had a complementary set of products and technologies that they were selling to a similar customer base that also served the Pay TV market.

So, my management team and the RF Magic team were able to convince our respective boards that we should join our companies and take the combined company public in 2007. It was a bold move for both boards; but we moved forward, and completed the acquisition by mid-2007.

The process of filing your S1 with the SEC is a lengthy process, and it was even more drawn-out due to the complexity of the merger between Entropic and RF Magic. We got the green light from the SEC to proceed with the IPO. Then, the day before we were scheduled to go on the IPO roadshow, one of our largest customers made overtures that they would cause problems for us if we did not give them a special deal. As a result, I spent the next four days working with that customer to resolve issues and clear the path for us to start marketing our deal to Wall Street.

However, by that time it was the week of Thanksgiving, and the US investors were unavailable to meet. So we decided to start marketing our deal in Europe the Monday after Thanksgiving at a price range of $9 to $11 per share. While we were in Europe, the sub-prime meltdown started to occur back home. Needless to say, this caused a lot of fear, uncertainty and doubt among public company investors. We spent two weeks on the road marketing our deal, visiting New York City twice, and a dozen other US cities. But the state of the market rendered us unable to get sufficient subscriptions to our deal to go public. It was a disaster.

The evening before we had planned to go public, we had a big conference call with my board, our bankers, lawyers and accountants to announce the bad news. I wanted to proceed with the IPO for a number of reasons, the most important being our need for additional cash to fuel our strategy and bolster our balance sheet. During this heated call, we made a team decision to try for one more day marketing our deal at $6 to $8 per share instead. We reduced the size of the offering from $100 million to $50 million.

The next day, the bankers, my CFO and I got on the phones "smiling and dialing for dollars." We were able to secure sufficient interest to get the company public at a price of $6 per share – and it quickly traded above $8 per share in the first day of trading. This was the best possible outcome under the circumstances. Raising this capital turned out to be critically important to the survival of the company during the economic downturn, without which we wouldn't have soared afterward.

Over the next four quarters, we consistently met our numbers as the public markets continued to melt down. Our strong balance sheet allowed us to weather the storm. Like 99 percent of the companies on the planet, we missed our earnings projections in Q4 2008; and the following quarter, our stock price went below our cash balance. And, at the same time we were working through the DirecTV re-design that that I discussed in Chapter 9 of this book. Needless to say, it was a very stressful time!

At the low point in Q1 2009, our stock was trading at 42 cents a share. But due to our decision to raise the money in the IPO, Entropic was able to weather the nuclear winter of the Great Recession, and emerge with massive deployments from DirecTV, Comcast, Time Warner Cable, Cox Communications, Rogers Cable, and a dozen other small cable operators using MoCA. We were also able to ramp our RF Magic business at DirecTV and Dish Network. In Q4 2011, Entropic had just completed a $100 million secondary offering, and was trading at over $11 per share, which was north of a $1 billion valuation. There were ups and downs after that, but I can say one thing for certain: anyone who invested in Entropic as a private company, who did not panic during the Great Recession, or get greedy when we hit $1 billion, made a lot of money. The main lesson learned here is that there will be ups and downs, highs and lows, and peaks and valleys in running a company, but as the leader of the company, you need to set the strategy, remain optimistic, execute like crazy, and drive the vision with conviction. Of course you need to constantly interpret what is happening in your environment, and adjust as appropriate. You must have a willingness to stick with things when times are tough in order to accomplish anything great!

I hope you have enjoyed this book, and that it has provided you with some practical tools and insights to help you create a fundable business plan and pitch for your startup. I hope you have found some of my stories entertaining and insightful, and they help you make better decisions, more often, and more quickly.

The ability to increase your "batting average" and speed of decisions – even by a few points – can be the difference between your startup's success and failure. Key decisions frequently require that you consider technical, business, political, and cultural issues. If you have a good idea as a starting point, drive a strong planning process, gain organizational commitment, and have a will to win, then the chances of getting your business funded and succeeding as a company improve dramatically. It will still be a lot of work, and gut-wrenching at times; but what the heck – you only live once!

Just remember: Be authentic. Be patient. Be persistent. Be honest. Be transparent. Don't panic! And remember to *PLAN COMMIT WIN!*

Recommended Resources

Article by Patrick Henry in *Entrepreneur*, "Why Some Startups Succeed (and Why Most Fail)," February 18, 2017 (https://www.entrepreneur.com/article/288769)

Article by Faisal Hoque in *FastCompany*, "Why Most Venture Backed Companies Fail," December 10, 2012 (https://www.fastcompany.com/3003827/why-most-venture-backed-companies-fail)

Article by Carmen Nobel in *Harvard Business School*, "Why Companies Fail – and How Their Founders Can Bounce Back," March 7, 2011 (http://hbswk.hbs.edu/item/why-companies-failand-how-their-founders-can-bounce-back)

Article by *Statistic Brain*, "Startup Business Failure Rate by Industry," January 24, 2016 (http://www.statisticbrain.com/startup-failure-by-industry)

Article by *CB Insights*, "Top 20 Reasons Startups Fail," December 26, 2014 (https://www.cbinsights.com/research-reports/The-20-Reasons-Startups-Fail.pdf#page=2&zoom=auto,-79,710)

Article by Paul A. Gompers, Anna Kovner, Josh Lerner, and David S. Scharfstein in *Harvard Business School*, "Performance Persistence in Entrepreneurship," July 2008 (http://www.hbs.edu/faculty/Publication%20Files/09-028.pdf)

Article by *Compass* in *Ecommerce Genome*, "Startup Genome Report," May 28, 2011 (http://blog.compass.co/discover-the-patterns-of-successful-internet/)

Article by Jason Nazar in *Forbes*, "14 Famous Business Pivots," October 8, 2013 (https://www.forbes.com/sites/jasonnazar/2013/10/08/14-famous-business-pivots/#66b2bcf35797)

Article by Paul Kedrosky in *Kauffman Institute*, "The Constant: Companies that Matter," May 10, 2013 (http://www.kauffman.org/what-we-do/research/2013/05/the-constant-companies-that-matter)

Article by *Practical Business Ideas*, "7 Reliable Sources of Business Ideas and Opportunities," July 26, 2015 (http://www.practicalbusinessideas.com/2015/04/sources-of-business-ideas-investment-opportunities.html)

Article by Eric Kutcher, Olivia Nottebohm, and Kara Sprague in *McKinsey & Co.*, "Grow Fast or Die Slow," April 2014 (http://www.mckinsey.com/industries/high-tech/our-insights/grow-fast-or-die-slow0)

Book by Michael Porter, *Competitive Strategy*

Book by Michael Porter, *Competitive Advantage*

Book by Peter Thiel, *Zero to One*

Book by Geoffrey Moore, *Crossing the Chasm*

Article by *Creative Survey Systems*, "Sample Size Calculator," March 9, 2017 (http://www.surveysystem.com/sscalc.htm)

Article by *Harvard University*, "Survey Questionnaire Design," February 25, 2016 (http://psr.iq.harvard.edu/book/questionnaire-design-tip-sheet)

Article by *Lehigh University*, "Conducting Focus Groups," September 2, 2002 (http://www.cse.lehigh.edu/~glennb/mm/FocusGroups.htm)

Data from the *US Census*, April 2, 2017 (https://www.census.gov/)

Article by *Wikipedia*, "Free Online Resources," December 13, 2016 (https://en.wikipedia.org/wiki/Wikipedia:List_of_free_online_resources)

Article by Eric Popkoff in *City University of New York*, "Methods for Effective Internet Research" (http://depthome.brooklyn.cuny.edu/economics/internetresearch.htm)

Article by Laura Kinoshita in *HubSpot*, "Avatar Workbook," (http://cdn2.hubspot.net/hub/18316/file-13370555-pdf/docs/customer-avatar-workbook.pdf)

Article by *Digital Marketer*, "Customer Avatar Worksheet," March 8, 2016 (http://www.digitalmarketer.com/customer-avatar-worksheet/)

Article by *MindTools*, "Porter's Five Forces," February 4, 2005 (https://www.mindtools.com/pages/article/newTMC_08.htm)

Book by Eric Reis, *The Lean Startup*

Book by Malcolm Gladwell, *The Tipping Point*

Book by Dale Carnegie, *How to Win Friends and Influence People*

Book by Robert Miller and Stephen Heiman, *Conceptual Selling*

Article by Michelle Sun in *Forbes*, "Decision Making: Tips for First Time Startup CEOs," August 3, 2016 (https://www.forbes.com/sites/michellesun/2016/08/03/decision-making-tips-for-first-time-startup-ceos/#6e4ba9d42905)

The *U.S. JOBS Act* (https://www.gpo.gov/fdsys/pkg/BILLS-112hr3606enr/pdf/BILLS-112hr3606enr.pdf)

Article by Amy Wan in *CrowdFund Insider,* "Title III Crowdfuding Becomes Legal on May 16, What it Does and What's Still Lacking," May 17, 2016 (https://www.crowdfundinsider.com/2016/05/85696-title-iii-crowdfunding-became-legal-on-may-16-what-it-does-whats-still-lacking/)

Article by Philip Birnbaum and Andrew Weiss, *University of Southern California Center for Effective Organizations,* "Competitive Advantage and the Basis of Competition," May 1994 (https://ceo.usc.edu/competitive-advantage-and-the-basis-of-competition/)

Article by Fernando Suarez and Gianvito Lanzolla in *Harvard Business Review,* "The Half-Truth of First-Mover Advantage," April 2005 (https://hbr.org/2005/04/the-half-truth-of-first-mover-advantage)

Book by Clayton Christensen, *The Innovator's Dilemma*

Article by *Investopia,* "Zero Based Budgeting, or ZBB Process," December 7, 2016 (http://www.investopedia.com/terms/z/zbb.asp)

Article by *Quick MBA*, "GE-McKinsey Market Attractiveness Matrix," December 8, 2002 (http://www.quickmba.com/strategy/matrix/ge-mckinsey/)

Article by Dave Lavinski in *Forbes*, "Business Plan Template: What to Include," July 18, 2013 (https://www.forbes.com/sites/davelavinsky/2013/07/18/business-plan-template-what-to-include/#135aa4397fc6)

Article by the *U.S. Small Business Administration*, "Writing Your Business Plan," March 31, 2016 (https://www.sba.gov/starting-business/write-your-business-plan)

Article by *Entrepreneur,* "How to Write a Business Plan," July 2, 2015 (https://www.entrepreneur.com/article/247575)

Book by Jim Collins, *Built to Last*

Book by Jim Collins, *Good to Great*
Book by Oren Klaff, *Pitch Anything*

Book by Jerry Weissman, *Presenting to Win: The Art of Telling Your Story*

Book by Jerry Weissman, *In the Line of Fire: How to Handle Tough Questions – When It Counts*

About the Author

Patrick Henry is a serial entrepreneur and the founder and CEO of QuestFusion, a San Diego-based consulting company that provides strategic guidance to entrepreneurs and startup companies. Patrick is the former CEO of Entropic Communications where he took the company from pre-product and pre-revenue to a successful IPO on NASDAQ, and an eventual $1 billion valuation. Patrick has raised over $200 million of equity capital for his companies, and executed on over $2 billion in M&A transactions. He is a regular contributor to *Inc* magazine, *Entrepreneur* magazine, *The Huffington Post*, and *FastCompany*. Patrick loves working with entrepreneurs on their most challenging problems. He also enjoys golf, tennis, fine wine, snow skiing, Angel investing, and spending time with his family. You can find Patrick on Twitter @QuestFusion.

Index

D

E

F

G

H

I

K

L

M

O

P

R

R and D Projects 134
reakthrough projects 132, 133, 134, 142
return on investment (ROI) 93, 94, 115, 116, 117, 142, 147, 158
revenue by region 77
revenue projections 28, 69, 94, 96, 102, 104, 117, 142
revenue ramp 93
risk 23, 40, 53, 61, 93, 111, 116, 133, 134, 164, 175, 177, 179, 184, 186, 187, 188, 202
risk assessment 179, 188
roadmap 44, 47, 59, 64, 80, 92, 93, 125, 128, 129, 133, 137, 141, 142, 144, 148, 151, 156,
      193
run-rate revenue 103

S

sales cycle 95, 101, 102, 103, 131, 136, 137, 142
sales funnel 35, 95, 100, 101, 103, 114, 117, 128, 131, 143, 153, 156
secondary market research 75
served available market 58, 68, 114
situation analysis 31, 57, 58, 59, 60, 63, 64, 76, 89, 91, 92, 100, 113, 114, 124, 139, 140, 144,
      146
smart ideation 26, 31
strategic partnerships 54, 135
strategic planning process 26, 31, 32, 33, 51, 52, 53, 54, 55, 56, 57, 61, 62, 64, 71, 85, 89,
      92, 94, 117, 123, 124, 139, 140, 146, 148, 150, 151, 154, 156, 160, 188
sub-prime 202, 203
sustainable competitive advantage 39, 40, 44, 51, 59, 67, 123, 129, 136, 148, 156, 158
SWOT Analysis 59, 87

T

TAM 68, 69, 70, 72
target customer 43, 53, 76, 99, 108, 116, 117, 156, 159, 174
target gross margins 104
target market 28, 43, 44, 51, 58, 63, 65, 66, 67, 68, 69, 71, 74, 77, 86, 87, 93, 98, 110, 143,
      159, 174, 187
teaching customer 43, 47, 48, 49
team 18, 20, 22, 23, 26, 27, 28, 29, 30, 31, 32, 33, 34, 35, 38, 41, 42, 48, 49, 52, 53, 56, 57,
      60, 67, 71, 72, 87, 88, 89, 95, 107, 115, 134, 141, 142, 144, 148, 149, 150, 152, 154,
      155, 156, 158, 161, 163, 164, 165, 166, 167, 168, 170, 171, 172, 173, 176, 180, 181,
      183, 184, 185, 188, 189, 192, 193, 195, 196, 197, 200, 201, 203
tops-down analysis 100
total available market 58, 68, 114
total product 64, 123, 125, 126, 127, 129, 135, 136, 140, 143, 148, 151
total product concept 126, 127
total value letter 130
track record 26, 34, 55, 56, 67, 88, 95, 156, 186, 188, 189, 191, 193, 195, 197, 200, 201

U

W

Z

Made in the USA
Lexington, KY
20 April 2017